Index on Censorship

Free Word Centre, 60 Farringdon Road, London, EC1R 3GA

Chief Executive John Kampfner **Editor** Jo Glanville **Associate Editor** Rohan Jayasekera **Assistant Editor** Natasha Schmidt **News Editor** Padraig Reidy **Online Editor** Emily Butselaar **Head of Arts** Julia Farrington **Head of Events** Sara Rhodes **Finance Manager** David Sewell **Curator** Klara Chlupata **Public Affairs Manager** Michael Harris **Fundraising Coordinator** Lizzie Rusbridger **Events Assistant** Eve Jackson **Sub-editor** Caroline Palmer **Interns and Editorial Assistants** William Clowes, Bogdan Dragos, Martin Dudas, Kat Javakhishvili, Ramin Namvari, Isobel Palmer, Mi Kyoung Park, Tena Prelec
Graphic designer Sam Hails
Cover design Brett Biedscheid
Printed by Page Bros., Norwich, UK

Volume 40 No 1 2011

If you are interested in republishing any article featured in this issue, please contact us at permissions@indexoncensorship.org

PLAYING THE LONG GAME

Jo Glanville

Over the past year, an increasing number of commentators in the US have lined up to critique the role of technology in political activism with a sober, and sometimes cynical, analysis of Web 2.0's impact on authoritarian regimes. So when the Tunisian government fell in January, followed by the popular uprising in Egypt, the response was much more muted than in the aftermath of the Iranian elections 18 months previously: technology was acknowledged to have played a part, in spreading news of the protests for example, but was given no starring role. Yet these unprecedented events were fuelled and facilitated by digital media. The invitation to the blogger Slim Amamou to join the interim government in Tunisia was one of the most remarkable acknowledgments of the role of digital activists in civil society, not to mention the symbolism of his appointment in a country that has stifled free speech for decades.

Technology continues to transform the culture of activism, but it's now popular to view it more cautiously as part of a long game. In this issue of Index on the impact of digital media, the Chinese commentator Hu Yong considers it part of 'a long-term revolution'. While new media brings unprecedented knowledge of closed societies – from the monitoring of the Egyptian parliamentary elections last November to the transparency of the secret services in Russia – there are no illusions about its limits. For a brilliant analysis of what can happen when there's too much blind faith in technology, read Danny O'Brien's account of the Haystack debacle (pp. 73-86).

What of the US's part in the long game? Its influence in pushing for internet freedom continues to be critical – and much criticised. The government's hot pursuit of WikiLeaks – from the subpoena on Twitter to the attempt to cut the whistleblowing website off from all financial support – has diminished its standing as a global champion for free speech (David L Sobel discusses the culture of secrecy in the US on pp. 29-35). Yet activists overseas were already extremely worried by the impact of Hillary Clinton's push for internet freedom on their grassroots work, as Ivan Sigal reports. He makes a strong argument for a more enlightened approach, pointing out the short-sighted interests that have been influencing government policy. Reports on the Obama administration's enthusiasm for introducing greater surveillance (as Evgeny Morozov discusses pp. 50-56) do not inspire confidence in US support for a free and open internet either. Morozov identifies a growing 'anti-cyber sentiment' shaping the US's agenda – from the FBI encouraging tech companies to build back doors into their software to the current move towards sidelining online anonymity.

Beyond cyberspace, and in keeping with Index's tradition of publishing the best literary new work, you can also read novelist Kamila Shamsie's gripping analysis of Pakistan's infamous blasphemy law, an exclusive essay by the acclaimed writer Dubravka Ugrešic and the first English translation of the bestselling biography of the celebrated Armenian-Turkish editor Hrant Dink. Index on Censorship would like to thank the BBC World Service Trust for its support towards this issue. Keep up-to-date with censorship stories on www.indexoncensorship.org ❏

Jo Glanville
40(1): 1/4
DOI: 10.1177/0306422011400797
www.indexoncensorship.org

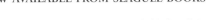

CONTENTS

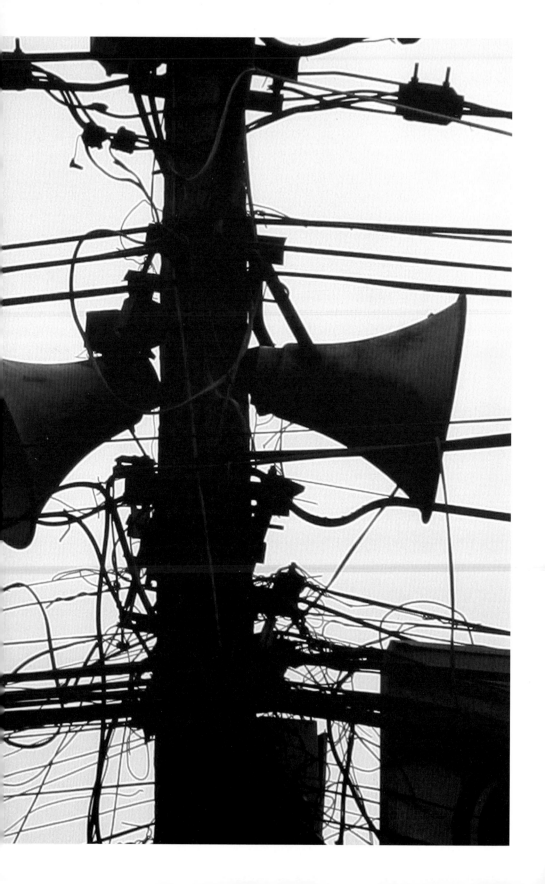

LIVING MEMORY   155

DISPATCHES

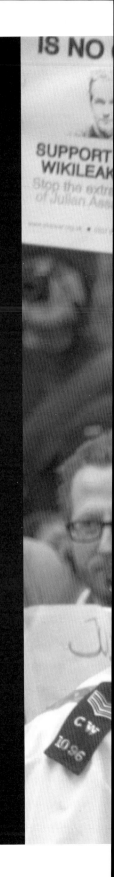

From WikiLeaks to
blasphemy: censorship news
on the front line

*Supporters of WikiLeaks' founder Julian Assange at
Westminster Magistrates Court, 14 December 2010
Credit: Andrew Winning/Reuters*

SPEAK NO EVIL

Pakistan's blasphemy law is a tool for persecution, says **Kamila Shamsie**. Its tyranny reflects the grip of religious extremism on political culture

I first became aware of Pakistan's blasphemy law soon before I turned 18. It was 1991, and although less than three years had passed since a plane explosion killed General Zia and subsequent elections brought Benazir Bhutto to power, the optimism which surrounded those events had already largely dissipated. Benazir's ineffectual government had lasted less than two years before being dismissed on corruption charges, and Zia's protégé Nawaz Sharif was the new prime minister. If Benazir lacked the political power and nerve to overturn any of the repressive laws which Zia had introduced or strengthened in the name of Islam, Nawaz lacked the inclination to do so. The coalition of parties which he headed – the Islamic Democratic Alliance – had, from the outset, knowingly positioned itself against Benazir's secular, female-led Pakistan People's Party.

So it wasn't surprising, but it was sickening, when Sharif's government went along with the Federal Shariat Court's ruling of October 1990, stating that an existing law which permitted life imprisonment rather than death to those found guilty of blasphemy was repugnant to Islam. 'The penalty for contempt of the Holy Prophet ... is death' the court plainly declared, and the government drew up a bill to bring the law into accordance with this ruling.

The blasphemy law, as it's come to be known, had been around in a milder form long before the Federal Shariat Court's ruling. In 1947, when the new nation of Pakistan adopted the Indian penal code (drawn up by the British), it included Section 295-A, which ran as follows: 'Whoever, with deliberate and malicious intention of outraging the religious feelings of any class of citizens of Pakistan by words, either spoken or written, or by signs or by visible representations or otherwise, insults or attempts to insult the religion or the religious beliefs of that class, shall be punished with imprisonment of either description for a term which may extend to three years, or with fine, or with both.'

For the first few decades of Pakistan's existence, 295-A was scarcely ever invoked, but when General Zia came to power following a military coup and decided the best way to circumnavigate the absence of a popular mandate was to claim the role of religious saviour, everything changed in the relationship between religion and state. 'Islamisation' became the word of the hour – or rather, of the decade that followed Zia's usurpation of power. All political parties were banned, their leaders imprisoned if they weren't in exile, except for the right-wing religious party, the Jamaat-e-Islami; advancement in the army and government became tied to a willingness to espouse Zia's Islam; school curriculums were 'Islamised' – which meant science fell out of favour, religious instruction was raised above all other subjects and the heroes of Pakistan's history were men who killed (usually Hindus and Sikhs) in the name of religion. It's worth noting that everyone in Pakistan today under the age of 40 who attended government schools (which is most of the school-going population) would have had Zia's curriculum and world view pressed into their brains from a very early age.

At the private school I attended, where we followed the 'O'-level syllabus and used English language texts published outside Pakistan, I grew up learning an entirely different version of the world. Our history lessons covered the ancient world, medieval Europe, a patchwork of Indian history from the Aryan invasions to the rise of Buddhism to the Mughals, through the British Empire to the creation of Pakistan. Islamic lessons – known, to the great amusement of my parents, as RI (religious instruction) – weren't given any great prominence, but at the same time all students knew that RI was the one lesson where you couldn't question anything.

Where did this attitude come from? I didn't learn it from my home life, I know; was it merely the atmosphere of Zia's Pakistan seeping through or had religion always been sealed in a protected bubble, except in the most radical circles? That's a question which requires more space to discuss – for the moment, suffice it to say that by the mid-80s an extremist version of Islam had not only been codified in law but had made its way into daily life. Moreover, the Soviet invasion of Afghanistan and India's acts of brutality against the largely Muslim population of the Kashmir Valley provided seemingly endless opportunities for pro-jihad propaganda. And then, of course, there was Saudi Arabia, delighted with the Wahabbism of Pakistan's new head of state and only too happy to spend its petrodollars funding Wahabbi mosques and madrassas in Zia's beleaguered nation.

All this is necessary to understand the atmosphere in which Zia widened the scope of the blasphemy laws, most notably with the addition of a new section 295-C: 'Use of derogatory remarks, etc. in respect of the Holy Prophet. Whoever by words, either spoken or written, or by visible representation, or by any imputation, innuendo, or insinuation, directly or indirectly, defiles the sacred name of the Holy Prophet Muhammad (peace be upon him) shall be punished with death, or imprisonment for life, and shall also be liable to fine.'

From the first, the new and expanded blasphemy laws were used as tools of persecution, used not only against non-Muslims but also against Muslims belonging to minority sects (who were viewed by the Wahabbis as being as bad as, if not worse, than non-Muslims). In an entirely skin-crawling manner, the newly fanged laws made perfect sense for Zia's rule – if you're going to claim that your authority stems from your role as champion of Islam, then you have to show yourself zealous in finding and punishing those who offend Islam, both at home and abroad. I have to confess that I don't recall any conversations around the blasphemy laws in Zia's days. Perhaps this is because there was so much else to froth at the mouth about around his Islamisation policy. Or because I was 13 at the time.

But I remember very clearly the terrifying period four years later, in the newly democratic Pakistan, when Nawaz Sharif's government did something which Zia's government had considered and rejected: impose a mandatory death sentence in blasphemy cases. Every hope that the end of Zia would see a reversal of his Islamisation policies died right there and the number of cases registered under 295-C kept on rising. Most of those who were accused, particularly in the early days, were non-Muslims or Ahmediyyas (a group who refer to themselves as Muslim but have been declared non-Muslim by the Pakistan state and are subject to vicious per-secution). But the case which most struck me was that of Akhtar Hameed Khan – a development activist, and one of the great heroes of Pakistan, and in particular of my home city of Karachi. I always heard his name uttered

Protest in support of the country's blasphemy laws, Karachi, Pakistan, 9 January 2011
Credit: Akhtar Soomro/Reuters

with admiration in my household, so it was chilling to pick up the newspaper one morning and find him accused of blasphemy, and even more chilling to hear the offending words were in a poem for children that 'could be read' as blasphemous if you chose to interpret them in a particular way. In the end, he escaped conviction (as he did on the other two occasions when he was accused under the blasphemy law), but the incident was enough to make it clear to me that the law could be used against any writer who strayed from orthodoxy.

In Benazir's second term in office, her government made some attempts to amend the blasphemy law to decrease its abuse by those seeking to persecute minorities or settle private scores. Her law minister Iqbal Haider later said he had won the agreement of other parties including the hardline religious Jamiat Ulema-e-Islam-Fazl (JUI-F) for making those amendments; but as soon as a newspaper erroneously reported that the government was planning to repeal the blasphemy laws, there were mass demonstrations by religious groups, which so intimidated the government that Iqbal Haider quickly declared support for the laws and dropped all talk of amendments.

It was around this time, while at university, that I first encountered the term 'Kafkaesque'. It seemed designed for the blasphemy laws: if one person had said something blasphemous, their words could not be repeated, not even to a policeman or in a court of law, because voicing the blasphemous words would itself be an act of blasphemy, and so the accuser would become the accused. Those charged under the blasphemy law were immediately imprisoned and placed in solitary confinement, awaiting trial, for their own protection; failure by the police to do so, the logic went, left open the possibility that the accused would be killed either by their neighbours (if they weren't imprisoned) or by other inmates (if they were imprisoned) because passions run so high over blasphemy charges. The only ray of light in all this was the refusal by the Supreme Court to uphold a single guilty plea in all the blasphemy cases that came before it, though in reality this could mean that an accused person could be in solitary confinement for years and years while the case worked its way through the judicial system. The judges themselves were not immune to pressure: in 1997, Arif Iqbal Bhatti, a High Court judge, was assassinated after finding three men not guilty of blasphemy.

The term Kafkaesque seemed designed for the blasphemy laws

At a certain point, it started to seem impossible to imagine anything would change. Attempts to merely modify the law had failed – President Musharraf had been the latest head of state to suggest the possibility, only to backpedal furiously in the face of pressure from the religious right. The growing feeling in Pakistan that Islam was a religion under threat in the world meant that there was even less likelihood than before of anyone mounting a challenge to the status quo.

Into this situation strode Salman Taseer, governor of Punjab (the most powerful province in Pakistan). In an entirely unprecedented move, he went with his wife to visit a Christian woman in prison, Aasia Bibi, who had been in solitary confinement for over a year after an altercation with a group of Muslim women, who had refused to drink from the same glass of water as her because they considered her 'untouchable'. These women later claimed Aasia Bibi had spoken blasphemous words in the course of the fight, and she was taken away to solitary confinement and later found guilty by the lower court.

Salman Taseer promised that Aasia Bibi would receive a presidential pardon. He also called the blasphemy law 'a black law' and pointed out that it was man-made, not God-made. President Zardari, whose backing Taseer claimed to have, started to dither. No presidential pardon was immediately forthcoming, and the judiciary (already at loggerheads with Zardari for entirely separate reasons) ruled that he had no right to grant a presidential pardon until the appeals process was exhausted. While Taseer continued to rail against the blasphemy law his own party deserted both him and Sherry Rehman, the already out-of-favour minister who had tabled a bill to amend the laws. The law minister, Babar Awan, insisted there was no possibility of changing the laws, and the interior minister Rehman Malik went one better and said that he would personally kill anyone who blasphemed. The right-wing press – who make Fox News look left-wing by comparison – applauded this stance and condemned Taseer.

'I was under huge pressure sure 2 cow down b4 rightest pressure on blasphemy. Refused. Even if I'm the last man standing' Taseer tweeted on 31 December. Four days later he was dead, gunned down by one of his own security guards, who said he did it because of Taseer's stand on the blasphemy law. For this, the murderer has become a hero in large parts of Pakistan – when he arrived in court to be arraigned, lawyers threw rose petals at him. Near the same time, Taseer's sons were throwing rose petals on their father's grave. Absent from the grave site was the head of Taseer's party, and the country's president, Asif Ali Zardari. It was clear that, rather than doing the only decent thing and repealing the blasphemy law in honour of Taseer's memory, the government wanted to put as much distance as possible between itself and the memory of the bravest man in its party.

It was left to Chaudhury Shujaat Hussain, a conservative politician from the Pakistan Muslim League (Quaid), to say that amendments were needed to prevent abuse of the blasphemy law. At the time, this seemed the best anyone could hope for – not to touch the law itself, but to make it very difficult for anyone to register an accusation of blasphemy against someone else. But even the faint hope of such procedural changes dimmed as the weeks went by. On 30 January, Hussain's political party and other centre-right parties joined the right-wing religious groups in a massive rally demanding that the blasphemy laws remain untouched. The head of the JUI (F) publicly declared that the newly appointed governor of the Punjab should visit Taseer's assasin in prison – just as Taseer had visited Aasia Bibi. A few days after this, Prime Minister Gilani announced that Sherry Rehman had agreed to withdraw her 'private member's bill' calling for amendments to the law, in keeping with the PPP's policy of leaving the law untouched. Politically isolated and under threat from extremists, Rehman – who weeks earlier had seen a 25,000 person strong rally march through her hometown of Karachi declaring her an enemy of Islam – said she would stand by her party's decision.

Through all this, the newspapers continued to carry stories of people charged under the blasphemy law, including a schoolboy who was reported to the authorities by an examination board for allegedly blasphemous remarks he had written on an examination paper. At the beginning of March, Pakistan's minorities minister Shahbaz Bhatti was assassinated and the Taliban claimed responsibility. He was a Christian and the only non-Muslim in the cabinet. In January, Bhatti had told AFP: 'During the Aasia Bibi case, I constantly received death threats. Since the assassination of Salman Taseer … these messages are coming to me even publicly. The government should register cases against all those using hate speech'. The Kafkaesque nightmare continues. ❐

©Kamila Shamsie
40(1): 14/20
DOI: 10.1177/0306422011399697
www.indexoncensorship.org

Kamila Shamsie's novels include *Burnt Shadows*, *In the City by the Sea*, *Kartography* and *Broken Verses* (Bloomsbury)

The Colonna Mediterranea monument by Paul Vella Critien, near Malta's International Airport, 12 April 2010
Credit: Darrin Zammit Lupi/Reuters

DO NOT DISTURB

Writers, journalists and even DJs are falling foul of Malta's censorious laws, reports **Charles Young**

The Pope's visit to Malta last year prompted international headlines for all the wrong reasons. The coverage focused on a group of locals who were becoming increasingly exercised over a monument on the exit route from the airport. The problem with the wooden structure was that its form was uncomfortably close to that of a phallus – although the artist denied that was what he intended. Should it be covered to save the Pope's blushes or should a diversionary route be mapped out? In the end it was left in place and the pontiff passed by without comment, but the incident comically illustrated a religious sensitivity on the island that can have more worrying consequences.

According to figures published by *Malta Today*, more than 9,000 people have been charged with blasphemy in the past five years. The offence carries a six-month sentence. In a country where 98 per cent of the population is Catholic, the law is still heavily influenced by the religion's moral code. Malta's constitution states: 'The authorities of the Roman Catholic Apostolic Church have the duty and the right to teach which principles are right and which are wrong.' The country's taste for censorship has attracted strong criticism from the Council of Europe. Films and plays are monitored by a government department known as the board of film and stage classification, nominally in charge of providing age ratings. It also has the power to 'ban and disallow' productions from being staged. Most other European countries gave up classifying theatrical productions years ago – the UK in 1968.

Malta's attitude to blasphemy, coupled with its antiquated obscenity laws, is creating a climate of censorship in the arts, with some worrying cases over the past 18 months. Last summer, a video DJ received a suspended sentence for displaying unacceptable images at a club night. As he was spinning his records, he projected an image of the Pope followed by an image of a naked woman. They were part of a sequence of images on a variety of themes. Unfortunately for the DJ, a policeman was among the clubbers and decided to charge him with both blasphemy and obscenity. The DJ, who has asked not to be named, has so far managed to keep his conviction from his employers as he believes he would almost certainly lose his livelihood if they found out. Last September, a culture minister demanded the removal of two photographs taken by a local photographer from the Gozo International Contemporary Arts Festival, as they were deemed to be explicitly pornographic.

But it's the recent ban on Scottish writer Anthony Neilson's play *Stitching* which has attracted particular concern. The play, about a couple's deteriorating relationship following the loss of their child, includes a scene where a character stitches up her own vagina. It was performed at last year's

Edinburgh Fringe festival with a 14 certificate. In Malta, it was deemed unsuitable even for adults and was banned in early 2009, just weeks before it was due to be performed. The censor board objected to some 'obscene' content and two blasphemous references.

The first of these comes in response to the statement: 'Sunday is the Lord's day', when one of the characters utters: 'Fuck him', while the other is an exclamatory 'Jesus fucking Christ'. In addition to blasphemy, the censors were offended by the play's 'obscene contempt for the victims of Auschwitz' – a charge which refers to a single line in which the male character claims that his first experience of masturbation was inspired by a picture of a naked Jewish woman in a concentration camp.

'Ironically enough,' says theatre director Chris Gatt, 'as they were saying this, a Jewish actress was getting plaudits in a Broadway staging of the same production and the *Jewish Chronicle* was reporting that.' Gatt was outraged by the censors' decision and was even tempted to defy them by staging the play and accepting the consequences.

The denial of truth is the negation of art and humanity itself

'I had declared a very public position that I did not believe there can be censorship of the stage,' he says. 'Theatre is about dialogue, I cannot permit the state or anyone else to stop that dialogue. Theatre has to have the ability to shock.' However, he later decided to challenge the ban via a civil action against the government. One of his witnesses was Neilson himself. 'I was angry but also amused, to some extent, I'll admit,' says Neilson. 'Such censorship is a denial of truth. Art is about reflecting the truth. If it is disallowed from doing so, art is little more than a state-sanctioned opiate. The denial of truth is the negation of art and, by extension, of humanity itself.'

The case against the government failed last summer when Mr Justice Joseph Zammit McKeon wholeheartedly endorsed the board's original findings, adding that even EU legal precedent had found that individual nations have a right to protect their own society's values. Malta joined the EU in 2004. The 82-page judgment makes sobering reading. At one point Justice

McKeon writes: 'It is unacceptable in a democratic society that a person is permitted to swear or utter vulgar words in public, even in a theatrical script. If this court permits this in a democratic society, it would be discriminating between those who are punished because they swear in public and those who are allowed immunity because they swear within the context of a play.'

However, as Gatt points out, this principle is applied inconsistently. 'The exact phrase ['Jesus Fucking Christ'] appeared over and over at the end of the film *Burn after Reading*, which was shown in Malta with a 16 certificate. Why is it suddenly objectionable in a play?' These inconsistencies frustrate artists but have galvanised them in their campaign. Strip clubs also appear to be flourishing on the island.

Gatt is appealing against Justice McKeon's findings in Malta but is resigned to losing again. He is prepared to take the case to the European Court of Human Rights where he has more cause for optimism. Malta's censorship regime would appear to breach the European Convention on Human Rights which states that 'freedom of expression … is applicable not only to "information and ideas" that are favourably received or regarded as inoffensive but also to those that offend, shock or disturb the state or any sector of the population'.

One of Gatt's witnesses was a Catholic priest, Father Abela, a member of the Church's own classification board, which publishes guidelines, separately to the state, as to which films it deems suitable for viewing by its congregation. Here was someone who, despite his clear Catholic convictions, believed the play should be performed uncut. Father Abela explains: 'It's not that you approve [of the content] but you understand it happens in real life. On stage you depict what happens in real life so you know what others are going through. The emotions are conveyed through these actions. You have to be careful when you start banning plays or films which are not to your liking when you are in power. What you do to others might be done to you in the future.'

In court, Father Abela's testimony was countered by the government's own holy witness and had little effect. He was then sacked from his position on the Church's own board.

There is a current court case which could prove a turning point in the future of Malta's censorship regime – this time in relation to written obscenities. As *Index on Censorship* was going to press, post-graduate student Mark Camilleri was due to discover his fate over a short story published in the October 2009 edition of the student magazine which he edits.

The story, 'Li Tkisser Sewwi' (Fix what you break), a graphic stream of consciousness in which a Maltese youth relates his sexual conquests and his attitude to women, fell foul of the country's obscenity laws. Malta's

Pornography and Obscenity Regulations of 1975 define obscenity or pornography as 'the exploitation of, or undue emphasis on, sex, or any one of the following subjects, namely, crime, horror, cruelty and violence' but in theory exempts works which are 'in the interests of science, literature, art or learning or other objects of general concern'.

This qualification echoes the UK's 1959 Obscene Publications Act which permitted obscene material 'providing that it is in the interests of science, literature, art or learning or of another object of great concern'. It was the 'literary merit' defence that acquitted Penguin, D H Lawrence's publishers, in 1960 at the *Lady Chatterley* trial.

Camilleri has to convince the court that he published a piece of literature rather than salacious material intended to titillate readers. When news of his case broke in Malta he appeared on National TV, claiming the work was no different from Irvine Welsh's novel *Porno* and others like it that were freely available in the university library. He also railed against the university rector who had originally reported him to the police.

However, the university defended its actions and promptly put its copy of *Porno* under lock and key. Whatever the outcome of Camilleri's trial – and he too will take his case to the European Court if convicted – it has already polarised public opinion and put the issue of censorship at the top of the news agenda.

The firebrand student – a relative term amongst Malta's politically apathetic youth – now heads a protest movement known as the 'Front Against Censorship' and regularly organises demonstrations and events to promote the cause. 'There are some politicians who play the game, politically, and do not offer an opinion about the issue because if you offer an opinion in favour of censorship you might be accused of being a conservative dictator,' he says. 'But on the other hand, if you say that you are against censorship you might be attacked for being a liberal leftist. So many politicians keep their mouth shut and play it safe.'

Some believe his style of campaigning has already proved counterproductive. The criminal code which covers obscenity legislation was amended in parliament soon after the Front formed. Anyone prosecuted today now faces a jail sentence of 12 months as opposed to Camilleri's potential six months behind bars.

He has, however, secured the support of opposition MP Owen Bonnici who, while a traditionalist on the issue of blasphemy, does believe the obscenity laws need re-drafting to protect literature and ensure authors aren't labelled as pornographers.

'I want to redefine the definition of porn to protect children and some sectors of society but want to give full liberty to artists because a healthy democracy needs artists and I really believe in the power of artists to change society,' he says.

But even a measured view, such as this, unleashed a torrent of abuse in the form of anonymous letters, which claimed Bonnici was doing the work of Satan. It's clear that he, Chris Gatt and Mark Camilleri need to play a sophisticated game in Malta if they want to have any influence.

Gatt believes that reform will ultimately depend on external factors, 'We are due to host a European Capital of Culture in 2018 and I don't think any European Commission will endorse this when there's a regime of censorship in the arts. So ultimately, by ten years' time, this should all be water under the bridge. If it isn't we'll have to stop performing. To perform under a regime of censorship is undemocratic and despotic.' ⌐

©Charles Young
40(1): 22/27
DOI: 10.1177/0306422011399822
www.indexoncensorship.org

Charles Young is a journalist and producer. His documentary about Mark Camilleri's campaign and trial will be broadcast on al Jazeera English on 5 April as part of its *Witness* strand

REX

Rex Features
Serving the world's media

We support free speech

www.rexfeatures.com

THE URGE TO CLASSIFY

With the Obama administration failing to honour its commitment to openness, leaks are of the few means of holding government to account, says **David L Sobel**

WikiLeaks' publication of secret US information, culminating with the release of thousands of diplomatic cables late last year, resulted in a firestorm of official criticism and predictions of dire consequences – both for American interests and for those responsible for the breach of secrecy. Secretary of State Hillary Clinton said the disclosures 'tear at the fabric' of responsible government and wanted to 'make it clear to the American people and to our friends and partners that we are taking aggressive steps' to hold those who leaked the documents accountable. Attorney General Eric Holder announced without elaboration that the US government has initiated 'an active, ongoing, criminal investigation with regard to this matter'. While the dimensions of that investigation are not yet clear, the Justice Department sought records from Twitter, and reportedly other social media sites, in an effort to trace the communications of individuals affiliated with WikiLeaks.

The unauthorised disclosure of sensitive information raises a host of controversial policy issues, including the proper scope and reach of US espionage laws, the inadequacy of existing protections for whistleblowers who seek to reveal improper or illegal government activities, and the sufficiency of security procedures employed by the diplomatic, intelligence and military communities. While all of these issues will be hotly debated over the coming months, the WikiLeaks disclosures highlight two longstanding and related problems that hinder the public's right to know about governmental activities – the overclassification of information and the failure of transparency laws to operate in an effective manner. Both contribute to an environment in which unauthorised disclosures are more likely to occur.

Excessive secrecy has long been a characteristic of bureaucracies, particularly those operating in the domain of 'national security'. But experience suggests that overuse of the 'secret' stamp can be counter-productive and actually weaken the protection of truly confidential information. As US Supreme Court Justice Potter Stewart famously observed in the Pentagon Papers case in 1971, 'when everything is classified, then nothing is classified, and the system becomes one to be disregarded by the cynical or the careless, and to be manipulated by those intent on self-protection or self-promotion'. And while 'everything' might not yet be classified, a great deal of information is. Daniel Patrick Moyhihan, who chaired the Commission on Protecting and Reducing Government Secrecy in the mid-90s, noted that, in 1995 alone, US agencies created roughly 400,000 new secrets at the 'Top Secret' level (the highest of three), a designation premised on the claim that disclosure would cause 'exceptionally grave damage to the national security'. The Moyhihan commission found that unnecessary classification was rampant and concluded that, '[e]xcessive secrecy has significant consequences for the national interest when, as a result, policymakers are not fully informed, government is not held accountable for its actions, and the public cannot engage in informed debate'. The commission proposed a series of recommended reforms, including legislative actions, most of which were ignored.

More recently, the official US commission established to investigate the terrorist attacks of September 11 reiterated that overclassification of information remains a serious problem; as Thomas Kean, the commission chairman, noted, 'three-quarters of what I read that was classified shouldn't have been'. The vice chairman, Lee Hamilton, observed that some estimates of the number of classified documents reach into the trillions and, echoing Justice Stewart, warned that 'an abundance of secrecy diminishes the attention paid to safeguarding information that really does need to remain out of the public's view'. There is no question that the security classification system is (to put it charitably) badly broken and that a vast amount of important, but innocuous, information is improperly withheld.

It is important to recognise that excessive classification on national security grounds is not the only impediment to official transparency. US agencies are also authorised under the law to resist disclosure of material for a wide variety of reasons. These include personal privacy, confidentiality of commercial data obtained by the government from private companies, protection of the government's 'deliberative process' and prevention of interference with law enforcement activities. Taken together, this panoply of rationales for official secrecy often frustrates the presumption of openness for which the US political system prides itself.

That presumption of transparency is embodied in the Freedom of Information Act (FOIA), which is premised, as the Supreme Court has recognised, on Congress's intent 'to permit access to official information long shielded unnecessarily from public view'. First enacted in 1966, the FOIA was strengthened in 1974 after the dangers of unchecked government power and secrecy were laid bare by the Watergate scandal. Despite its lofty objectives, the law has been plagued by administrative processing delays; while the statute requires agencies to respond to information requests within 20 days, such requests often languish in a bureaucratic limbo for months or years. FOIA implementation has also been impeded by a knee-jerk bureaucratic tendency to push the limits of the narrow statutory exceptions that permit the withholding of requested material, and reluctance on the part of the courts to hold government agencies to the law's strict disclosure requirements. In sum, the FOIA has not proven to be an effective antidote to overclassification and excessive secrecy. As history has shown, the absence of orderly and reliable procedures to ensure a free flow of important official information invites and encourages unauthorised leaks, whether the Pentagon Papers in 1971 or the WikiLeaks archive today.

When Barack Obama took office as president in January 2009, he identified transparency as one of the highest priorities on his agenda for change. On his first full day in office, Obama issued two sweeping proclamations concerning transparency. The first announced that the new administration 'is committed to creating an unprecedented level of openness in Government'. The second mandated that 'the Freedom of Information Act should be administered with a clear presumption: in the face of doubt, openness prevails'. Lest there be any question about the manner in which his administration intended to operate, Obama directed that '[t]he government should not keep information confidential merely because public officials might be

President Barack Obama carries a classified intelligence summary, Washington DC, September 2009
Credit: Scott Applewhite/AP

embarrassed by disclosure, because errors and failures might be revealed, or because of speculative or abstract fears'.

As we enter the third year of the Obama administration, there is a consensus within the US transparency community that the president's early promises remain unfulfilled. One of the first tests of the highly touted commitment to openness came when Obama was urged to reverse a Bush administration decision to remove certain White House records from the reach of the FOIA. Despite the fact that several administrations, both Democratic and Republican, had entertained FOIA requests prior to the restrictive Bush policy, and in stark contrast to the promise of an 'unprecedented level of openness', the Obama White House refused to revert to the earlier, more transparent practice. While the administration has taken several steps to open some of its activities to greater scrutiny – disclosure of the names of official White House visitors being the most prominent example – these initiatives have fallen short of the far-reaching promises Obama trumpeted as he came to office.

FOIA requesters and open government advocates have compiled a long list of cases in which efforts to use the legal disclosure process to pry loose official information have proved fruitless – even after the purported pro-transparency Obama policies were put in place. One recent case, in particular, illustrates how the improper withholding of requested information can encourage unauthorised leaks. In late 2009, a FOIA request was submitted to the Department of Justice for an internally-produced history of the department's Office of Special Investigations (OSI), the unit responsible for excluding or deporting Nazi collaborators who entered the United States illegally or fraudulently in the years following the Second World War. Preparation of this historical report was commissioned by former Attorney General Janet Reno in the late 1990s and was completed in 2006. The Justice Department withheld the 600-plus-page report in its entirety, asserting that the document was a 'draft' and that disclosure would harm the agency's 'deliberative process'.

After a court action was initiated to challenge the withholding decision, the department released a heavily redacted version of the report, in which roughly a quarter of the contents were blacked-out. The controversy caught the attention of the *New York Times*, which began investigating the matter. Ultimately, the full, uncensored text of the Nazi-hunting report was leaked to the *Times*, which published it on its website and featured some of its more notable revelations in a front-page article. While some of the officially withheld information was mildly embarrassing (the *Times* article was headlined, 'Nazis Were Given "Safe Haven" in US, Report Says'), most of it was innocuous and much of it was already in the public domain. A comparison of the leaked report with the censored version released under the FOIA revealed that the Justice Department sought to conceal large amounts of information that had previously been disclosed in congressional hearings, court proceedings and, ironically, articles published in the *New York Times* and other newspapers. Even after the leaked report became public, the department continued to withhold the 'official' version for two months, finally relenting and releasing the document, with very minor deletions, just days before it was scheduled to justify its actions in court.

One of the most troubling aspects of the OSI history episode is that the agency responsible for the improper withholding of information was the Justice Department, which was charged by President Obama with the responsibility of ensuring compliance with his directive that a 'presumption of openness' should govern all official disclosure decisions. Further evidence of the department's failure to embrace that presumption came during an oral argument before the Supreme Court in January. When asked by the justices whether the government agrees with longstanding Supreme Court precedent requiring that FOIA exemptions be 'narrowly construed' in order to advance the statute's presumption of full disclosure, the high-level Justice Department attorney arguing the case unequivocally rejected the notion. 'We do not embrace that principle,' he told the visibly bewildered justices.

The Obama administration's failure to act in a manner consistent with its pro-transparency rhetoric has dashed the hopes of many in the open government community and has done little to alter an environment in which unauthorised leaks of 'sensitive' information are often the only means of bringing sunshine to official activities. Excessive secrecy cannot be overcome by a FOIA process that all too often gets bogged down by bureaucratic delay and improper withholdings. As such, the climate in which the recent WikiLeaks disclosures have occurred is not very different than the one that prevailed in 1971 when Daniel Ellsberg felt compelled to disclose the secret history of the Vietnam War contained in the Pentagon Papers. In 1989, some 28 years after he presented the government's case for suppression of the Pentagon Papers before the Supreme Court (and predicted dire consequences if the material was disclosed), former Solicitor General Erwin Griswold wrote a confessional post-mortem for the *Washington Post:*

> I have never seen any trace of a threat to the national security from the publication. Indeed, I have never seen it even suggested that there was such an actual threat.... It quickly becomes apparent to any person who has considerable experience with classified material that there is massive overclassification and that the principal concern of the classifiers is not with national security, but rather with governmental embarrassment of one sort or another. There may be some basis for short-term classification while plans are being made, or negotiations are going on, but apart from details of weapons systems, there is very rarely any real risk to current national security from the publication of facts relating to transactions in the past, even the fairly recent past. This is the lesson of the Pentagon Papers experience, and it may be relevant now.

It is likely that a similar assessment will one day be made of the WikiLeaks revelations. In the meantime, Justice Stewart's prescient observation that when everything is stamped 'secret' no information can truly be protected continues to ring true. ❐

©David L Sobel
40(1): 29/35
DOI: 10.1177/0306422011401974
www.indexoncensorship.org

David L Sobel is Senior Counsel at EFF's Washington, DC office, where he directs the FOIA Litigation for Accountable Government (FLAG) Project. David has handled numerous cases seeking the disclosure of government documents on privacy policy and challenges to government secrecy. He has been inducted into the First Amendment Center's National FOIA Hall of Fame

Protesters wave an Egyptian flag, Tahrir Square, Cairo, 29 January 2011
Credit: Yannis Behrakis/Reuters

DAYS OF ANGER

The revolution in Egypt is unprecedented but not
unexpected, says **Salwa Ismail**

The sustained mass protests that began in Egypt on 25 January lit the spark of revolution in a country long subject to repressive rule. The scale of the protests, the resilience of the protesters and their firm resolve to bring down the regime represented an unprecedented movement in Egypt and come as a wonderful corrective to the unfounded view of Egyptians as politically apathetic. For more than a decade now, Egypt has been witnessing increased levels of collective action involving broad segments of society. Between 1998 and 2008, industrial workers mounted thousands of protests, numerous strikes and sit-ins. The textile workers revived their long-established tradition of activism, best exemplified by 10,000 workers of the Misr Spinning and Weaving Company in al Mahala al Kubra going on strike in 2008. There have been newcomers on the scene of public engagement and action as well, most notably the tax collectors who staged an 11-day occupation of central Cairo demanding better pay, also in 2008. Alongside this mobilisation for economic change, other groups in society organised and pressed for political reform. In April 2006, in a widely publicised and well-regarded move, a group of prominent judges held a sit-in led by the Judges' Association to denounce electoral fraud in the 2005 elections. The regime responded with punitive measures, bringing a number of the judges before disciplinary panels to sanction them. Subsequently, judicial oversight of elections was repealed in the constitutional amendments of 2007.

These high-level and well-organised activities have been complemented by spontaneous popular activism for basic rights. In towns and villages throughout Egypt, ordinary people have gathered to protest against poor infrastructure and police abuse. Stand-offs between the people and the police have often ensued, sometimes ending in violence.

In a sense, Egypt was building up to, and possibly rehearsing for, a showdown with the regime. Although the revolution is unprecedented, it was not entirely unexpected. The early activism and the ongoing mass protests have succeeded, in a remarkable way, in breaking down the wall of fear erected by the police over many years. To appreciate the magnitude and significance of these events, we should consider the kind of restrictions that were imposed on any expression of opposition to the regime and its policies. A web of regulations and decrees has encircled Egyptian citizens, undermining their capacity to organise and act collectively.

Although Egypt formally has a multi-party system, it has been dominated by one party for 35 years. The National Democratic Party (NDP), headed by Hosni Mubarak until his resignation from the post in early February, maintained a monopoly position in state institutions and government. To maintain this dominance, the regime devised regulations that made it virtually impossible to challenge it on a level playing field. These regulations set restrictions on the formation of political parties through a committee, affiliated with the shura council (the upper house of parliament) and comprising prominent NDP figures. Political parties in formation like the al Wasat party (formed by a dissident group of Muslim Brothers members) and the al Karama party (formed by a dissident group of Nasserist party members) were refused legal recognition on several occasions and their appeal to the Supreme Administrative Court was rejected in 2007. Existing parties have also been given little space to manoeuvre: they were subject to security oversight intended to limit any outreach to constituents or to the wider public.

As the National Democratic Party resorted to electoral fraud, elections increasingly lost their relevance for participatory politics. Vote rigging, buying of votes, violations of electoral rules and the use of thuggery at election time were the norm and reached a flagrant level in the parliamentary elections last November, in which the NDP won 93 per cent of the vote. It is worth noting that the NDP leadership introduced measures to prevent its own members from running as independents if they do not win party nominations. The party introduced the novel, and possibly unique, practice of devising nominations lists with multiple NDP candidates for the same seat. The November elections were therefore run primarily as a contest among NDP members.

In a sense, parliamentary contests and the continued dominance of the NDP were elements of the consolidation of the extensive executive powers concentrated in the hands of the president. The 1971 constitution, and subsequent amendments, invested the president with absolute authority over key institutions (e.g. as commander of the armed forces, and head of the Supreme Council which oversees judicial organisations), with rights to appoint and dismiss the prime minister, his deputies and cabinet members. In 2007, amendments to the constitution effectively foreclosed the possibility of non-NDP candidates running for the presidency. According to Article 67, nominations to the presidency required the endorsement of at least one-third of the members of the People's Assembly. The nominee who won one-third of the votes of assembly members would become the candidate for the post of president of the republic and the candidacy referred to the people for election (or, more properly, ratification) in a plebiscite. Needless to say, with an absolute majority in the assembly, only NDP-supported nominees would become candidates for the presidency.

While the formal political structure and the institutions of political participation were closed off, emergency laws have further undermined ordinary citizens' civil rights. These laws have been in effect since Mubarak came to power in 1981 and allow administrative detention without trial on the order of the minister of the interior. Under detention regulations, imprisonment does not issue from a court order, nor does it follow a court order of arrest. Rather, people are arrested at the police officers' discretion and detained for months or years. Once the police have submitted a report to the security division, claiming that a particular individual constitutes a threat to national security, an internment order can be issued by the Ministry of the Interior. The detention rules deny civil liberties and guarantees of due process and leave citizens at the mercy of the police.

The Egyptian police departments govern vast areas of social life. They have responsibilities for security and public order, but also include jurisdiction over the regulation of outdoor markets, the use of public utilities such as electricity and the implementation of municipal building codes. With regular outdoor market raids and campaigns to monitor citizens' use of these utilities, the police have intruded into the daily life of ordinary citizens. Endowed with the arbitrary powers of emergency laws, the police have engaged in extortion, and used violence to intimidate and silence any questioning of their powers.

The police have carried out numerous types of policing campaigns, maintaining continuous monitoring and surveillance of the population. Within the remit of what is called 'traffic committees' (*lijan murur*), they randomly stop drivers to verify driving licences or identity cards, and to inspect cars. Similarly, 'security committees' (*lijan amniya)* target drivers and pedestrians and subject them to investigation procedures. Security checks and roadblocks on the streets of Cairo and many other cities have been part of Egyptian citizens' daily reality. Young men, feared by the regime for their potential for activism and resistance, have been the main target of these practices, particularly those living in low-income neighbourhoods, and they are commonly stopped and asked to present their identity cards; following inspection, they may be hauled into the police station and subjected to what is known as 'suspicion and investigation procedures' (*ishtibah wa tahari*). This involves detention in the police station for up to three days while the police verify whether or not the detainee has a criminal record.

These practices are aimed at the control of the population, undermining Egyptians' ability to challenge the police and ultimately the ruling regime. Indeed, in response to these practices, ordinary citizens have devised means of avoiding dealing with police. For example, young men

Protesters calling for the resignation of President Hosni Mubarak, Tahrir Square, Cairo, 1 February 2011. Credit: Suhaib Salem/Reuters

from low-income neighbourhoods refrain from frequenting areas with roadblocks and checkpoints. Furthermore, women have stepped in as intermediaries with the agents and agencies of the state, including the police. I have noted in my work on the politics of everyday life in Cairo that women process applications for utilities services, negotiate fines issued by the police for violations of rules relating, for instance, to the use of electricity utilities, or for unauthorised occupation of public space by vendors in the informal markets.

The police's arbitrary powers have been exercised with impunity under the emergency laws, which include the power to detain without charge individuals who are deemed a threat to national security. In the 80s and 90s, these provisions were applied, in the first instance, to suspected Islamist militants, but by the late 90s, they were used by the police to silence any questioning of their abuse of power and their engagement in illegal activities. It is estimated that the number of administrative detainees reached 30,000 in the late noughties. In addition to the use of systematic torture of suspects in police stations, the police engage in monitoring and surveillance and use a large number of informants and thugs. Indeed, the police have hired thugs, used them as informants in low-income quarters of the city and rewarded them with licenses to operate kiosks or run minibus services.

Protests became the only means of voicing demands

Under conditions such as these, organising for political reform, and social and economic transformation, using traditional channels and within existing institutions, became an increasingly fruitless exercise. Ordinary citizens and activists were aware that elections were not likely to change the regime, but were rather a means for achieving its consolidation. Analysts interpreted the results of the elections last November as laying the groundwork for the succession of the president's son Gamal to the presidency. The absolute majority of the NDP in parliament, secured through unfair and illegitimate tactics, appeared certain to guarantee that only the party elite's candidate would be nominated, and the prevalent speculation had been that Gamal Mubarak was the person of choice. Emergency laws were extended until 2012 and the politics of security was intensified, aided by constitutional amendments that introduced new anti-terrorism laws in 2007, in effect normalising emergency rule.

Protests became the only means of voicing demands and expressing opposition. In 2009 and 2010, various groups organised sit-ins in front of the National Assembly and the Council of Ministers with the objective of making representations to parliament and to the cabinet. These actions were often dismissed and the protesters' demands sidestepped. Given that opposition political parties had their hands tied, civil society organisations, youth groups and broad short-term coalitions coalesced around demands for change. Activists of diverse social and political backgrounds agreed on the importance of ending Mubarak's presidency and thwarting plans for his son's succession. The movement of Kifaya (Enough) as well as the National Association for Change emerged to express these demands, organising protests focused on free and fair elections, and open democracy. They have a core group of activists, but participants in their events remained small in number.

The broadening of the agenda for change came with the first call for a general strike by textile workers on 6 April 2008, which drew wide attention and support from a cross section of society. A group of young activists formed what has come to be called the 6 April youth movement (*shabab sita ibril*) in support of this call, using the internet to organise and develop ideas about the course and direction of change. The movement's website provides a virtual space for discussion and for the circulation of information. Using Facebook, the movement publicised events and mobilised its social circles. Importantly, the activists and supporters of the movement were open to members of diverse political groupings including the youth wing of the Muslim Brotherhood. A brief survey of their website reveals that their concerns are focused on broad social issues of equality and social justice, and on the protection of freedoms and civil liberties. These broad demands are articulated along with a vision for open and representative political government.

The protection of civil liberties is central to the youth movement and independent political activists: the level of abuse and humiliation of ordinary citizens by the police has been a catalyst in mobilising people. Human rights organisations have documented widespread cases of torture in police stations and the severity of the situation has acquired greater publicity following specific cases. A well-organised campaign against torture has also sensitised the public to the severity of the abuses. In 2006, a video was circulated on YouTube showing police abuse that shocked Egyptian society.

The video, recorded by the police on a mobile phone, showed police officers severely beating and sexually abusing a young male minibus driver, Imad al Kabir, from the Greater Cairo quarter of Bulaq al Dakrur. Last year, the murder of Khaled Said, who was dragged out of an internet cafe in Alexandria by two policemen in civilian clothes and violently beaten to death, further escalated concerns. The 'We are all Khaled Said' group that formed in 2010 has captured the indignation of citizens who have come to fear for their own security, in a society where the rule of law is disregarded. Khaled Said became one of the iconic figures of the unfolding revolution.

Citizens' daily experience of humiliation on the streets, the growing social disparities – whereby a small elite has monopolised the wealth and resources of the country – and the blockage of formal political avenues, have all been factors driving the organisation of independent opposition to the regime and the widespread mobilisation to bring it down. The unfolding revolution in Egypt began when the 6 April youths called for 'a day of anger' on 25 January, using Facebook and their website to publicise the call. On 18 January, in a powerful video message, Asmaa Mahfouz, one of the group's founders, addressed her fellow citizens, particularly young men, to join her in public protest. In a moving and emotional speech, she underlined that they all had a responsibility to take part and that their success or failure depended on acting together. In her video log, she summed up the collective desire for liberty and dignity in the following statement: 'I'm making this video to give you one simple message. We want to go down to Tahrir Square on 25 January. If we still have honour and we want to live in dignity on this land, we have to go down on 25 January. We'll go down and demand our rights, our fundamental human rights. I won't even talk about any political rights... We want our human rights and nothing else.'

It is too early to provide a comprehensive account of all the factors that have contributed to the people's uprising and to the revolution. The media and analysts have both emphasised the role of social media in building up networks of dissidents and facilitating the organisation of protests. Some have credited the 'Facebook generation' with lighting the spark of collective action. Undoubtedly, social media activists put the tools of virtual communication to remarkable use in calling for 'the day of anger'. However, events can only be understood if we look at the experience of the vast majority of Egyptians over the last three decades under Mubarak's rule.

It was fitting that the revolution had its spectacular beginning on Police Day and that the young took the lead in breaking down the barrier of fear that the police have erected over a long period of time. Egypt's youth has bravely come forward, along with broad segments of society, to reassert their right to dignity and freedom. They have taken the first steps towards exercising fully the responsibilities of citizenship. It is in reference to these objectives that the protesters' main and most powerful slogan, 'the people want to bring down the regime', should be understood. The desired change is nothing short of an overhaul of the institutions and structures of government.

©Salwa Ismail
40(1): 36/45
DOI: 10.1177/0306422011402456
www.indexoncensorship.org

Salwa Ismail is professor of politics with reference to the Middle East at the School of Oriental and African Studies, University of London and author of *Political Life in Cairo's New Quarters: Encountering the Everyday State* (University of Minnesota Press)

THE NET EFFECT

EFFECT

The limits of
digital freedom

TAMING CYBERSPACE

As the US government pushes for increased surveillance online, **Evgeny Morozov** considers the political interests at stake in bringing the internet under control

Given all the unabated enthusiasm about what the internet could do for grassroots movements, it's easy to forget that it is the paranoia of the US government, concerned that its communication networks might not survive a nuclear stand-off with the Soviet Union, that we have to thank for the internet's existence.

Ironically, five decades later, another fit of paranoia – also originating from America but increasingly common in other countries – is now shaping the future of the internet. The growing anti-cyber sentiment is easy to explain: most governments assume – some on good evidence – that the internet has helped to accelerate the seamier side of globalisation, enabling child pornographers, Islamic terrorists and internet pirates to find each other and collaborate, Wikipedia-style.

This is definitely not what most policymakers expected. For much of its existence, the internet was viewed – at least in America – as little else but a commercial platform. Predictably, the early designs of internet infrastructure sought to optimise business innovation, rather than the ability of law enforcement agencies to listen in on conversations conducted online.

During the so-called crypto wars of the early 90s – when the government, the academy and the industry engaged in a protracted public battle about the benefits and perils of encrypted communications – the government lost. Washington was persuaded that secure communications are essential to commerce and that building back doors into computer systems would only compromise security. Since so much software and hardware (not to mention early internet standards) originated in the US, the opinions of other countries did not really matter. However, in 1994, all telecoms carriers became obliged to enable interception under a new wiretapping law, and this was extended to broadband network and Voice-over-Internet-Protocol (VoIP) services ten years later.

Today, America is considering taking further steps that will allow it to monitor all forms of online communication. The *New York Times* has reported that a bill is likely to be introduced this year allowing sweeping new regulations. Why the shift? National security concerns play a part: the terrorists who organized the attacks on Mumbai in 2008 famously used BlackBerries to communicate. There is also a growing concern about cyber warfare, with cyber-security contractors painting the risks associated with cyber attacks in extremely dark apocalyptic terms, if only to increase the amount of public funding that is likely to flow to their coffers to mitigate it (and such scaremongering is only likely to increase in the wake of high-profile but highly ambiguous cases like Stuxnet, a complex piece of malware that can target industrial infrastructure). Powerful firms in the entertainment industry, unhappy with the proliferation of online piracy, influence the agenda as well.

So far, governments have been trying to tame the internet by passing on the costs of identifying and removing unwanted content to for-profit intermediaries like internet service providers (ISPs). This, however, does not work in all cases and ISPs are not happy to take on extra responsibilities. And, in some cases, they simply can't: Research in Motion (RIM), the company behind the BlackBerry, manages and stores all communications of its users directly, bypassing the ISPs. Clearly, this is something that governments do not like, especially given that in most cases RIM's servers are not in their jurisdiction.

After several governments – India, Saudi Arabia and the United Arab Emirates – complained, RIM has expressed willingness to negotiate. Even though details of their particular arrangements with each country are not publicly known (and in the case of India they seem to be still ongoing), it's likely to have empowered governments rather than users. RIM's willingness to compromise has already been noticed by other governments, who are now beginning to impose their own, often unrelated, demands: in January, RIM

Indonesia, August 2010. In January 2010, BlackBerry's Research in Motion agreed to the Indonesian government's demands to block BlackBerry users from accessing pornography Credit: KeystoneUSA-ZUMA/Rex Features

agreed to Indonesia's demands to block all BlackBerry users in the country from accessing pornography.

Although the US government has been able to intercept Voice-over-Internet-Protocol (VoIP) services since 2004, services like Skype remain difficult to crack because of encryption. It may become possible if tech companies are forced to build back doors into their software – a solution that is currently being actively pushed by the FBI, in talks with leading firms in Silicon Valley. In the long run, this solution is likely to hurt the interests of America's technology industry, as foreign governments would probably be wary of using American software that is likely to feature back doors leading to the offices of the National Security Agency. This may explain why so many foreign governments are touting open-source technologies: since their code can be audited, the odds of them containing a secret back door are, on average, lower.

Another, more extreme, solution is to radically re-engineer the internet and grant the US government one giant back door to virtually everything. The latter solution seems technologically burdensome as well as commercially and politically untenable, as it would, in theory, also give foreign governments easy access to American communications. But since many US politicians – led by Senator Joe Lieberman – are longing for some kind of an internet kill-switch that would allow the government to shut down all online communications in case of an emergency, the idea of re-engineering the internet probably has more support than appears on first sight. Sadly, Lawrence Lessig was probably right when he remarked that it would take an i-9/11 for the government to pass an i-Patriot Act. As far as most American politicians were concerned, the release of the diplomatic cables by WikiLeaks came very close to being this i-9/11.

Another solution is to grant the US government one giant back door

One way to avoid the increased government oversight would be for users themselves to encrypt all their online communications, so even if the software they use contains secret back doors, governments wouldn't be able to do much with the encrypted data that they intercept. Leaving aside some technical quibbles (e.g. it's not clear how such a solution would work with a Skype-like service), this is unlikely to work in the long run. If anything, this may push governments to simply ban the use of encryption tools; given that in many countries (and especially in authoritarian ones), governments also happen to own or control internet service providers, enforcing such a ban on 'encryption by default' may not prove all that challenging. In the interim, authoritarian governments would simply be blocking anonymity-enhancing tools like Tor, something that is already happening in Iran (where the main ISP also happens to belong to the Revolutionary Guards).

But governments are as interested in learning more about discussions that are conducted in the open as they are about conversations that are hidden. The Fort Hood military base shooting in 2009, the Tucson shooting in January and the failed transatlantic underpants bomber, Umar Farouk

Abdulmutallab, all left a sizable public trail of hints and tips online prior to committing their crimes. Data-mining systems that scan social media for any signs of potential aggression are poised to be embraced by law-enforcement and intelligence agencies to identify emerging threats.

Not surprisingly, the American government is a pioneer here already: back in 2009, In-Q-Tel, the venture capital arm of the Central Intelligence Agency, invested in Visible Technologies, a social media tracking firm, and in 2010 it made another investment in Record Future, a similar service that tracks relationships between people, organisations and events. While most of these systems are mostly used to track trends rather than spot particular individuals, such technology is likely to improve and allow for zooming in on particular individual cases.

To get a glimpse of what's coming, one just needs to look at a handful of existing semantic search engines like Silobreaker and Maltego: these services provide several layers of context that are not available on Google (for example, highlighting companies or organisations that a search target may be affiliated with). Such services are only poised to improve, as it's primarily developed to satisfy the needs of the financial sector; Wall Street is pouring millions into developing social media and news-trackers to identify stock trends. It's only a matter of time before similar methods are deployed against organisations or individuals.

The main obstacle here is that once suspicious content has been identified, governments would still have a hard time linking it to particular individuals as long as they don't use their real names when posting online. One obvious way to overcome this is to require users to use their real names, tying their online accounts to their existing national identity numbers or some other form of identification (for example, this is already a common practice in South Korea and it may soon be gaining in popularity elsewhere).

Speaking at a Stanford University event in January, Howard Schmidt, White House's cyber-security coordinator, announced that the American government would be considering ways to introduce a universal online identity as well, emphasising that it would be optional rather than required. However, it's not clear for how long such a scheme would be able to remain truly 'optional': there are real benefits that accrue to users from disclosing who they are and where they are. Will service providers even bother with anonymous users if they present inferior opportunities for advertising? That so much online communication is now shifting to mobile devices is yet another reason to worry about the future of anonymity: since they have to connect to towers, mobile phones are the easiest devices to trace.

American efforts to tame cyberspace look particularly troubling when contrasted with Washington's publicly announced plans to promote 'internet freedom'. When some representatives of the US government seek to remake the internet to make it easier to spy on its users, while others complain about similar impulses in China or Iran, this makes the US government look extremely hypocritical. After all, it's very hard to build an argument as to why the Chinese law enforcement agencies shouldn't try to build backdoors into Chinese software when Americans are building backdoors into their own software.

Given Washington's excessively nervous reaction to the WikiLeaks saga, any moves by the US government with regard to internet freedom will now be watched with increased suspicion around the world. Sadly, growing global efforts to oppose America's desire to dominate the internet may also delegitimise those parts of the internet freedom agenda – for example, addressing the growing challenge to freedom of expression posed by the spread of denial-of-service attacks – that look perfectly reasonable. ❐

©Evgeny Morozov
40(1): 50/55
DOI: 10.1177/0306422011399696
www.indexoncensorship.org

Evgeny Morozov is the author of *The Net Delusion* (Public Affairs). He is a contributing editor to *Foreign Policy*, a visiting scholar at Stanford University and a Schwartz fellow at the New America Foundation

SAQI BOOKS
Understanding the Middle East in Revolt

VYING FOR INFLUENCE IN THE NEW EGYPT

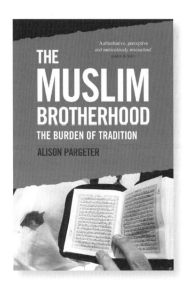

The Muslim Brotherhood: The Burden of Tradition
Alison Pargeter

'Alison Pargeter has established a reputation as one of the best current analysts of Islamic radicalism. This book – detailed, authoritative, sober, perceptive and meticulously researched – shows why. It is an important contribution to our understanding both of the Muslim Brotherhood itself, to the controversies that surround the movement and to the broader phenomenon of political Islam. A must read for scholars, students and anyone interested in the Middle East.'
Jason Burke

£20 | 978-0-86356-475-8

EXAMINING THE DEMOCRACY DEFICIT IN THE ARAB WORLD

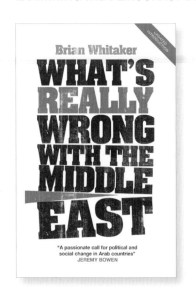

What's really wrong with the Middle East
Brian Whitaker

'A passionate call for political and social change in Arab countries' Jeremy Bowen

'[Should] be required reading by Arab elites from the Atlantic to the Gulf' *Al Hayat*

'A passionate attack on the corrosive effects of inequality' *New Statesman*

£10.99 | 978-0-86356-624-0

www.saqibooks.com

TOOLS OF RESISTANCE

Ordinary Egyptians made their voices heard around the world during the uprising – in spite of the government's clampdown on the internet. **Jillian C York** reports

In the Arab world, internet censorship is the norm. Only a handful of governments have managed to avoid the temptation of filtering political sites and social networks from the public view. Until the end of January, Egypt had one of those governments, content with surveillance and occasionally arresting bloggers, but never denying access.

Following the popular uprising, that ceased to be the case. On 26 January, just 24 hours after demonstrations began, Egypt placed a ban on Facebook, effective across all internet service providers (ISPs). The following day, the target was Twitter, and on the next, the entire internet.

The government's decision to shut down the internet is a clear indication that it recognised its potential threat: prior to the start of the demonstrations, Egyptians with both internet and political savvy had been leveraging their online networks to coordinate protests, undoubtedly coupled with offline action. Popular Facebook groups, such as 'We Are All Khaled Said', became rife with activity. At one point, a Google document was posted to capture the contact information of group members in case of a Facebook ban. Few suspected the ban would extend to the entire internet.

A senior army officer salutes a crowd of protesters at Tahrir Square, Cairo, 29 January 2011
Credit: Yannis Behrakis/Reuters

From the 28th through to the 31st, one plucky internet service provider, Noor, remained connected. Amongst its customers were journalists and local activists who tweeted as much as they could, sharing information from phone calls with friends on the streets. Egyptian 'geeks' quickly mobilised to figure out dial-up connections and posted details to blogs.

And then, early on 1 February, Noor – that last outpost of connectivity – was taken offline as well, leaving Egyptians, and by extension much of the world, in the dark. Without reports from the streets, many observers were at a loss, unsure of which media outlet to trust. Google and Twitter quickly issued a joint announcement, detailing a new service that would allow anyone in Egypt to dial an international number and leave a voice message that would then be echoed to the world via Twitter. Though the service got a number of calls and the international community quickly translated tweets from Arabic to English, the lack of internet meant that there was little anyone could do to ensure Egyptians found out about the initiative.

Of course, without the internet, the protests went on. Despite the ban on SMS and mobile networks, thousands poured into Tahrir Square and in public spaces around Egypt. As the internet returned on 3 February, some proclaimed that they were drawn into the streets precisely *because* of the shutdown; without the ability to write and share with the world what was happening, they chose to become a part of it.

Despite the ban on SMS and mobile networks, thousands demonstrated

Though the internet may never be the straw that breaks the camel's back, its role shouldn't be understated. Take, for example, a Google document posted to Facebook on 22 January. That document – like its paper cousin, a pamphlet circulated on the streets of Cairo – shared logistical information, such as what to do in the event of tear gas, and where to gather in downtown Cairo. But unlike its paper cousin, it cost nothing and could be updated in real time, collaboratively, making the life of its creator easier. The same could be said for Facebook: once a political organiser might have picked up the phone some 30 or 40 times, now a Facebook update can reach thousands. Incidentally, an update for the protests scheduled for 28 January received 400,000 responses.

It is not just organising, but the dissemination of information that makes the internet so key in times of unrest. In Tunisia, protests proliferated for nearly three weeks before the international media took notice, but that didn't stop Tunisian internet users from reporting. Citizen journalists filled in the gaps by posting photographs to blogs, uploading videos to Facebook, and yes, tweeting. As the media began reporting on the unrest, they recognised the value of these local reporters, and often used their updates as primary sources. Al Jazeera in particular played a unique role with its ability to broadcast – via satellite – back into Tunisia, often including social media in its reports.

The return of Egypt's internet on 3 February coincided with horrific violence, mostly from paid pro-Mubarak thugs. Though by that time the media had descended on Cairo, as the sun set and reporters retreated to their hotels for the state curfew, it was the brave protesters, mobile phones in hand, who were able to report from the streets. And it was their voices – the voices of ordinary Egyptians – that were heard around the world. ❏

©Jillian C York
40(1): 57/60
DOI: 10.177/0306422011402279

Jillian C York is a researcher and blogger who focuses on internet censorship in the Middle East and North Africa

CAPTIVATING, MOVING, EVOCATIVE

JEFFREY MOORE

The
Extinction
Club

'A fantastic genre-bending tour de force, as sophisticated as it is brutal'
Heather O'Neill, author of *Lullabies for Little Criminals*

Route to revolution

Digital activism has long been a way of life in Egypt, reports **Ashraf Khalil**, from monitoring political corruption to protesting against police brutality

Egypt has always been one of the fastest and most enthusiastic cultures in the Middle East to embrace technology. Activist Egyptian bloggers such as Wael Abbas made their reputation by posting incendiary videos showing endemic police brutality and the use of torture in interrogation. In at least two cases, evidence of torture was circulated online and led to the prosecution of police officers. 'Now everyone can see what's happening in the police stations. That's something that touches a nerve in ordinary citizens who are not political activists,' Abbas says. One Egyptian online activist created the 'piggipedia' http://www.flickr.com/groups/piggipedia, a Flickr account showing a gallery of senior Egyptian police officers photographed at demonstrations. The murder of Khaled Said in Alexandria last June became a new rallying point for protest, after he was beaten to death in public, in front of witnesses, by plain-clothes police officers. Autopsy photographs of his badly battered face circulated immediately on the internet, sparking a month-long round of demonstrations and vigils – many of which were organised and announced on Facebook and Twitter. The Facebook group 'We are all Khalid Said' later became a hub for the January uprising.

The internet was already well established as a virtual meeting point for evading the country's harsh laws against political activism under President Hosni Mubarak. In 2008, a 30-year-old civil engineer named Ahmed Maher created a Facebook group called the 6 April Movement to commemorate the date of a violent clash between police forces and a group of striking textile factory workers in the Nile Delta city of Mahalla al Kubra. The page then took on a life of its own, gathering more than 70,000 members and expanding beyond labour activism to encompass all manner of political activity. 'We can't have a proper headquarters. It's not like we can just rent an office,' Maher says. 'But on the net there are groups like ours meeting 24 hours a day.'

Last March, employees at the popular online news site Islam Online went on a mass strike to protest against editorial interference by the site's management. The strike was broadcast over the internet thanks to a live feed on Bambuser, the video-streaming website. In addition to documenting the chants and vigils, many strikers used the streaming video feed to give testimonials directly to viewers.

Before the uprising in January, active bloggers such as Ahmed Maher and Wael Abbas were shifting their energies to Twitter and other online platforms. The appeal, they say, is a new level of interactivity and the creation of a virtual community. Abbas, in particular, has employed his Twitter account in a novel way. After years of posting videos that embarrassed the government, he would be detained, questioned and searched while leaving or arriving in Egypt. On at least one occasion, the authorities confiscated his laptop. As a result, whenever Abbas headed to the airport, he would tweet the news to his 5,000 followers. If he was detained or questioned, he would tweet that as well and the Egyptian online community would immediately rally behind him. In early February, as the Tahrir Square uprising was entering its second week, Abbas was arrested, questioned and released.

The parliamentary elections last year were the first to receive digital scrutiny. Anyone following #egyelections on Twitter was deluged with information from the estimated 44,000 polling stations spread across 29 governorates. Activists, journalists and election monitors all posted and forwarded the latest updates and pictures from around the country. If a monitor or a journalist was turned away from a polling station by police, the incident was instantly posted or tweeted. When Sobhi Saleh, a Muslim Brotherhood-affiliated MP, was attacked in Alexandria, the news circulated through Twitter so fast that journalists and human rights workers were able to interview him in hospital.

'When a new report came in from our reporters in the field, the first thing I would do is put up feeds on our Twitter account, before I even posted the news on the website,' says Lina Attalah, co-managing editor of the English edition of *al Masry al Youm*, Egypt's largest independent daily newspaper.

President Hosni Mubarak's ruling National Democratic party won more than 90 per cent of the vote in a victory that generated widespread condemnation and allegations of voter intimidation, strong-arm tactics and old-fashioned ballot box stuffing. The electronic evidence posted on Twitter, Facebook and YouTube amounted to a damning and comprehensive dossier of the day's injustices.

Until the uprising in January, activists like Maher and Abbas would express frustration at the inability of Egypt's robust internet political scene to translate into mass demonstrations. Most Egyptian protests would still amount to the same group of people invariably surrounded by central security riot police. But that's all history now. ❐

©Ashraf Khalil
40(1): 62/64
DOI: 10.1177/0306422011399690
www.indexoncensorship.org

Ashraf Khalil is Index on Censorship's Middle East regional editor. He is based in Cairo and writes regularly for *The Times*, *Wall Street Journal* and *Rolling Stone* magazine, Middle East edition

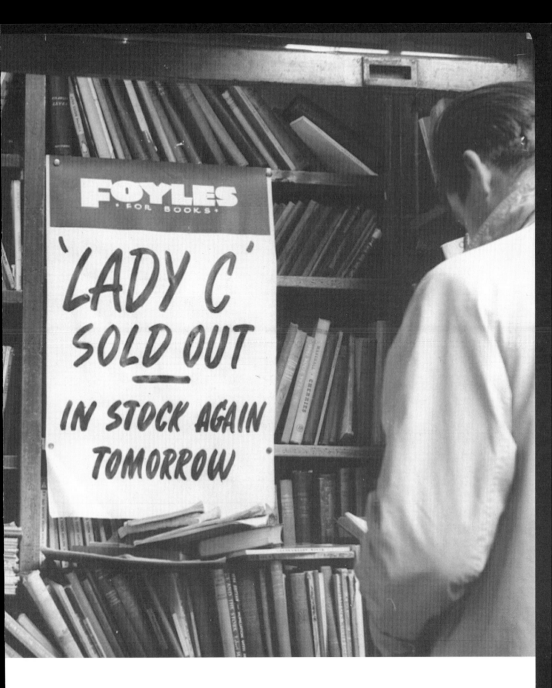

Making voices heard
since 1903

A crowd mourns the victims of a fire in Shanghai, 21 November 2010. Microbloggers uploaded videos and photos of the disaster and called for people to gather at the site
Credit: Aly Song/Reuters

CROWD CONTROL

Microblogging is changing the face of activism in China. But don't expect a revolution, says **Hu Yong**

Last November, one of China's largest internet portals, Sina, held the country's first conference for microblog developers in Beijing. It announced that the number of users on its microblog service had reached 50 million by the end of October, with users publishing 25 million messages every day. Most are young – 47 per cent are 22 or younger – while 57 per cent of active users are female.

Fifty million users is a milestone. Take a closer look at the speed at which Sina's microblogging platform has developed: on 28 August 2009, the service opened for public beta testing. Sixty-six days later it had more than one million users; a year later, this figure had rocketed to 30 million. In the four months leading up to that landmark figure, an average of five million new users were joining monthly, rising to ten million a month in the autumn of 2010. Growth had become explosive.

Meanwhile, the other major portals were opening up their own microblogging platforms. Microblogs became a nationwide craze, just as blogs had been before them – only microblogs were easier to start, faster and more interactive. In Taobao, China's largest e-commerce portal, people even began to trade followers – one follower could be bought at a price range of 1 jiao to 1 yuan (10 yuan = US$1.5). An advertisement from a Taobao retailer bragged about the extent and influence of the medium: 'When you have 100 followers, you're an office memo; when you have 100,000, you're a city newspaper; when you have 100 million, you're national television.' Imagine 100 million netizens, each with their own microblog. How would freedom of speech and action on China's internet, and even in Chinese society, be expanded?

In 2010, microblogging services in China grew exponentially. The amount and frequency of information and the connectedness of users went far beyond that of any other online application. A series of events over the year demonstrate its impact:

During the Yushu earthquake and the Zhouqu landslide 140-character messages were used to pass on information, express sympathy and offer assistance.

A well-known campaigner and microblogger accused a former senior executive of a multinational of faking his academic credentials – leading netizens to pursue the issue of diploma mills and honesty amongst the business elite.

When members of the Zhong family of Yihuang in Jiangxi immolated themselves in protest at a forced relocation last September, others in the family attempted to reach Beijing to speak to the media but were prevented from boarding their flight by local government employees. Reporters microblogged the stand-off live, while the family used the same method to plead for help from netizens. The incident drew nationwide attention and the government officials involved were removed from their posts, opening a new page in the history of human rights defence in China – microblogging rights defence.

On 15 November last year, 58 people died in a fire in an apartment building in Shanghai. As the building burned, observers used their cameras and phones to take and upload images to microblogs. On 20 November, microbloggers called for the people of Shanghai to visit the scene to mourn and lay wreaths – and the next day, 200,000 citizens did so. Both through the live broadcast of events and the mass laying of wreaths, this new medium brought people together and played a major role in the government's handling of the incident.

These events display the nature of microblogging: individual, instant and interactive. But crucially, it is not only China's netizens who have mastered this – government and the media also use it, as a tool to poll public opinion or a channel of communication with the people. Looking back over 2010, we can see that a politics of microblogging has taken shape. It is an ideal medium for breaking news, an open platform for expression, an instrument of political participation and discussion – and an indispensable channel for open governance.

Fifty million users is a milestone. Growth is explosive

As microblogging makes its impact in China, we should pay our respects to the founders of Twitter. The creators of this instant media identified two basic human needs – to express ourselves and to follow others – and combined the two perfectly. We should also remember China's first microblogging platforms, such as Fanfou – they fostered China's first microbloggers in the first half of 2009, and it was these pioneers that allowed the Twitter-style service to expand as it has today. Twitter was officially blocked in July 2009 following the ethnic riot in Xinjiang and soon afterwards its most famous Chinese clone Fanfou was also closed down, leaving one million registered users homeless. When the major portals, including Sina, Sohu, QQ and Netease developed microblogging platforms and employed swarms of technicians and monitors to enforce propaganda orders, the new platform had a chance to flourish. The authorities still exert control however by switching some of the largest and most popular micro-blogging websites in China to 'beta' or 'testing' versions and sometimes shutting them down temporarily for 'maintenance'.

What does microblogging mean for China? It is a gathering place for citizen journalism, allowing local news to become national. It is a home for public discourse, a national arena that transcends place and class as never before. It is the source of citizen action, where the people unite and struggle together to improve society. In sum, microblogging has massively strengthened the public spirit of China's netizens – as shown in the emergence of the 'online crowd'.

The last few years have seen China's netizens act as online crowds for events happening anywhere in China by forwarding information, commenting and organising support and assistance during various public incidents. They have also taken action offline, such as the various action groups that sprang up during the widely reported Deng Yujiao case, when a hotel worker was charged with murder, and acted as trial observers or offered legal assistance.

With the arrival of Web 2.0, the idea that these online crowds can change China has become current in the media. The Chinese term for crowd has a derogatory connotation: it is the unfeeling gawker who watches distress and does not move to help. But the internet era has given the term new meaning. I think of this as a process of 'watching while participating, sharing while commenting': comments on online news articles, copying blog posts, forwarding tweets and texts, even posting articles, photos and videos on social networking sites. There are different methods, with different functions, but each simple click is equivalent to a democratic vote. One or two clicks from one or two people might not get any attention, but they add up and form public opinion.

The power of this kind of crowd comes from two sources. First, it's the power of witness. A young academic Liu Wenjin has said, 'In modern society our original sin is not ignorance, but ignoring.' The desire to observe scares those who prefer to act unseen. Spreading the truth on the internet is a form of testimony, taking information to the place where it can have the greatest effect.

Second, there is strength in numbers. Citizens use this to unite, to share and to work together or start some public action. The artist Ai Weiwei has said that there's no other way to melt the glacier, bar the total body heat of the Chinese people. These crowds are one way to donate your thermal energy to that task.

Ultimately, this crowd politics will create the 'micro-power' that pushes Chinese society towards improvement. This challenges the simplistic but common assumption that citizen activists can use social media to mobilise rapidly and change society on a large scale. In fact, social change will be more subtle. Václav Havel, an advocate of gradualist politics, often used concepts such as the 'politics of anti-politics', 'power of the powerless' and 'civic initiatives'. Collectively, it will require a movement of people who make the leap from thinking of themselves as subjects to considering themselves citizens.

Why is micro-power important? In the past, a small number of very motivated people working with unmotivated masses often led to disappointment. The activists could not understand why the people weren't interested, and the people could not understand why those obsessives couldn't just keep quiet. But today, keen activists should concentrate on a lower threshold for action – allow those who object a little to participate a little – and when all those efforts are combined, they will have real power. One postcard, one phone call, one coloured ribbon, one wreath – they can all add up to a powerful cry.

Artist Ai Weiwei says there's no other way to melt the glacier

The nature of micro-power is, as well-known blogger Ran Yunfei has repeatedly said, a constant advance of pawns to ultimately win the game. In a 1996 article 'The Difficult Russell', the historian Zhu Xueqin explained: 'The Chinese habit is either to rebel, or to surrender. We either rise up in open revolt, or submit unwillingly. What is lacking is the tenacity of spirit to neither foment rebellion nor to accept defeat, but to sustain patient opposition and make gradual advances. As a member of the Fabian Society, Russell advocated an inch-by-inch approach, becoming neither rash not discouraged, risking neither rapid advances nor defeat. Faced with bad government you may not achieve checkmate in a decade – but you move your pawns forward everyday.'

So micro-power has opened a series of small mobilisations and protests for China. It is not revolutionary and not about overthrowing the government – it is about a constant and gradual push along a long road of change, allowing all Chinese people more dignity and a more just society. So, in this sense, if we say that micro-blogging can change China, it is sure to be a long-term revolution.

In the diverse actions of countless people, China's future is gradually unfolding. These actions may be borne of courage, faith or empathy. Each time anyone – no matter who – stands up to defend their ideals, acts to improve another's fate, or opposes injustice, they send out ripples of hope. These ripples join and ultimately form a torrent which will wash away the dams of oppression, misunderstanding, enmity and indifference.

©Hu Yong
40(1): 66/71
DOI: 10.1177/0306422011399840
www.indexoncensorship.org

Hu Yong is an associate professor at Peking University's School of Journalism and Communication, and a founding director of the Communication Association of China (CAC)

~~TRIPWIRES~~

Freedom of expression is important, but are there limits?

Free speech can open up debate, or it can offend...

Where do **YOU** draw the line?

Index on Censorship's new youth programme in partnership with Phakama

www.tripwires.org

INDEX
ON CENSORSHIP

Phakama

STORM IN A HAYSTACK

Keeping secrets can be dangerous. **Danny O'Brien** tells the cautionary tale of an anti-censorship program that didn't live up to its spin

It's late July 2009: the contested Iranian election was over a month ago, but the protests against the result continue inside and outside Iran. I'm sitting in a San Francisco bar, empty and in the middle of the afternoon, with Austin Heap, the man behind 'Haystack' – a new system that he says will allow Iranians to evade internet censorship.

Since almost the very beginning of the crackdown in Iran, Heap had been a prominent figure in what the papers were calling a 'Twitter revolution': working from San Francisco to distribute proxies, single internet addresses to machines outside Iran that Iranians could use to evade their own country's net censors.

The proxies are quickly blocked, which is why Heap has been talking about a system that couldn't be blocked, a new system that would hide its anti-censorship efforts as efficiently as a needle is hidden in a haystack.

Heap is in his late 20s, but looks younger. He's thin and fast-moving, with a mop of unruly, San Francisco hipster hair. He says that he wasn't much involved in (international politics) before being caught up in the Green movement's online plight. He says he hasn't slept much for weeks.

He suggested this dim and dank bar instead of meeting at my office. I don't understand why. Our conversation is going around in circles.

'I won't open source the code,' he says, again. I look down at the scribbled notes on a napkin, where Heap explained the principles behind Haystack. It's a complicated plan. I can follow his talk of a three-tier network, local HTTP proxies, and polymorphic binaries. I'm not technical enough to write such a program, but even I can see it'll require a great deal of complex code.

I repeat once again to him that I don't care if he doesn't want to publish the source code, the blueprint to his program, publicly and openly. I'm just recommending somebody with expert knowledge privately check Haystack's code for errors that might make its users vulnerable.

Heap's solo stand against a government that I can already see is rapidly developing its own technical expertise is worrying me. His software is specifically for Iranian activists: it's almost certainly going to come under intense scrutiny from the Iranian authorities. They'll try to break its disguise, and learn as much as they can about its users.

Cracking the security protections in software requires thinking in perverse and non-obvious ways. If you've written the code yourself, and you don't have a background in computer security, you don't have the distance to consider the truly perverse ways others will abuse it. You need to have an external audit from those who can think in such twisted ways.

At the time, I was working for the Electronic Frontier Foundation (EFF), the first internet civil liberties group. Its founders were hackers, engineers, entrepreneurs and, famously, a songwriter for the Grateful Dead, John Perry Barlow. To say that the EFF has worked with computer security experts would be an understatement: it's kept them out of jail and trouble for two decades. As part of my work, I've run into the best in the United States: academics who have found flaws in the supposedly perfect computer security systems built by Sony, e-voting machine manufacturers and ATM makers; commercial organisations that Google and Microsoft use for this kind of work; brilliant and idiosyncratic individuals with hipster hair, cyberpunk pseudonyms and a taste for secret meetings in San Francisco dive bars like this. Given the good intentions of the Haystack project, I say, we could sort out a pro-bono deal with whichever is most compatible.

But Heap doesn't want to show anyone I recommend the code. It's okay, says Heap, I have had people look over the code. In Washington DC, he says,

Demonstrations following the contested presidential election, Tehran, June 2009
Credit: Omid Salehi

with a little nod to signify I should get what he means. He travels there a lot, he says. Very high level people.

He thinks that this will reassure me. I can see his confusion when my face falls.

Does Austin Heap know what he is getting himself into?

When Heap hinted that the US government had checked out his secret code, I wasn't fearful that Haystack has been compromised by American intelligence. My worry was Heap's judge of character, knowledge of history and his instincts about what secrets to tell, and when, and how.

The people Heap was showing the code to weren't spooks or spies. They were bureaucrats. Their job is to prevent countries like Iran getting hold of secure encryption products.

In that, they are about three decades too late. Allow me to export to you the secret of high-class encryption products right now, from the comfort of this New York hotel room, to wherever you are reading this in the world:

```
#!/bin/perl -sp0777i<X+d*lMLa^*lN%0]dsXx++lMlN/dsM0>j]dsj
$/=unpack('H*',$_);$_=`echo 16dio\U$k'SK$/SM$n\EsN0p[lN*1 lK
[d2%Sa2/d0$^Ixp'|dc`;s/\W//g;$_=pack('H*',/((..)*)$/)
```

Put that into a text file on your computer, and ask your local techie to turn it into an executable file. You now have a basic working encryption product that is, in principle, unbreakable by any known actor on the planet, from the server farms of Google to the secret machinery of the US National Security Agency.

From the 1970s onwards, the American government worked to prevent that secret from leaking out to the wider world. They classified that stream of apparent gobbledy-gook as a munition, and promised to punish anyone who exported it just as severely as if I'd smuggled them a tank or a tear-gas cannister.

The original plan to prohibit strong encryption from leaving the United States failed, partly because you can write the spirit of it in three lines of computer code; partly because, as the EFF successfully argued in court, prohibiting the dissemination of particular ideas, even if expressed in code, is against the First Amendment.

But mostly because, as the US State Department has recently found to its cost with WikiLeaks, it's very hard to keep a secret from the world once it is in digital form. In 1991, a copy of a complete implementation of strong cryptography written by American programmer Phil Zimmerman, Pretty Good Privacy (PGP), was uploaded onto the internet. Within hours, it permeated the US border. The US pressed for charges against Zimmerman, but it was too late.

Digital data was made to be copied. It doesn't matter if you try to classify it as a munition or put classified in capitals at the top. Its true nature is to be copied, and at almost every opportunity, that's what will happen.

Are there no secrets left, in an internet age? Well, clearly there are a few. There appear to be key facts about constructing nuclear weapons that don't make it onto the pages of Wikipedia. I've told precious few people about the conversations in this article before now. The code for Haystack remains to this day on a few people's hard drives, unreleased and unseen. Even in the internet age, you can keep a secret – if you don't put it on a public computer, if you keep it to a close set of completely trusted individuals, if you scribble it on note paper, or memorise it like a password and then wipe it from your hard drive.

No matter what your commitment to transparency and free expression, secrets matter. Even when you're fighting for the right to communicate freely, like Austin Heap, even if you're fighting for the free flow of all information over the internet, tell the wrong people your secrets and you're in trouble. And keeping the *wrong* things secret can break you.

Thanks to the legal battles over cryptography and a change of heart during the Clinton administration, you and I can now effectively talk about strong crypto as much as we want. You can only be punished if you smuggle strong cryptographic code to America's Axis of Evil – Syria, Cuba, North Korea, Sudan. And, of course, Iran.

Somebody must have told Heap prior to our meeting, correctly, that because Haystack had strong cryptography in it, he needed export permission from the United States government. As part of that process he'd shown them the code.

But that's just the beginning of Haystack's problems in getting its code to Iranians. Long before the election unrest, companies like Microsoft and Google started blocking downloads of their instant messenger clients in Iran – not because of the Iranian governments' restrictions, but because of the remainder of the United States' targeted sanctions against the Islamic Republic. In 2009, the blockade of exports to Iran was so universal, so exhaustive, it included tools of free expression. If you gave an Iranian a program that helped them speak to the rest of the world, from the land of the First Amendment, you could be criminally prosecuted.

If you gave an Iranian a program you could be criminally prosecuted

This is why, in 2009, people didn't share with the US government the secret code they intended to send to Iran to help liberate net users from censorship. It was the US government's stated policy to stop them.

Heap declined to let others see the secrets of the Haystack code in July 2009, but his project was anything but a secret for the next year. Every few weeks, it seemed, a new media outlet would rediscover Haystack and its photogenic, easily encapsulated figurehead.

When he won the *Guardian's* MediaInnovation award for Haystack in March 2010, the newspapers' photographers took pictures of him in moody 'genius hacker' poses, tied up with the cord from a computer mouse. Heap accepted the award for devising a program 'to protect the identities of Haystack's users [and] made it possible for people on the ground in Iran to reach blocked sites safely and securely, to organise inside the country and communicate with the world'.

When *Newsweek* ran a feature story on him in August 2010, they talked about how he was a 'computer savant', who had 'learned his first programming language in fourth grade'. Haystack was, it said, 'a step forward for activists working in repressive environments.'

Heap did not seek out the publicity he was gathering. But he didn't need to: it was too easy a story to write. He set up a non-profit to collect donations to the cause of developing his program. Money was donated. Hundreds of people sent him USB memory sticks to load up with Haystack's client software and smuggle into Iran.

Meanwhile, the Iranian Green movement passed into its second year of fighting a determined and increasingly technologically sophisticated opponent. Curious to see how Heap's plans were progressing, whenever I spoke with an Iranian activist, I asked them: do you use Haystack? When coders working on other anti-censorship programs met, they asked me and each other the same question: do you have a copy? Does anyone have a copy?

No one I met had a copy. In Haystack's absence from the Iranian opposition movement it was supposed to be built for, gossip began to spread: that the big secret about Haystack was that there *was* no Haystack. Just a request for donations, a publicity machine and the opaque Austin Heap.

Heap didn't seem like a conman to me. On the contrary, when we had met he seemed heartbreakingly sincere. But he continued to keep all the wrong secrets. He was getting publicity for Haystack (and asking for donations), yet refusing to reveal exactly what he was doing. He was asserting a strong stance against the Iranian government's meddling on the internet, but making no secret that he would do so while working with United States politicians and the State Department.

His plan to gain a licence for Haystack succeeded with great publicity in March 2010; the granting of such a licence was alluded to by Secretary

Clinton in an interview with Bloomberg TV 'because we think it is in the interests of American values and American strategic concerns to make sure that people have a chance to know what is going on outside of Iran'.

Mostly though, Heap seemed determined to keep Haystack secret from the very people who could help him the most: other computer experts.

When we met in July 2009, Heap accepted my invitation to speak at a public meeting on Iran and the internet. I also invited Jacob Appelbaum, a computer security research who had worked on Tor, another anti-censorship system already in use in Iran. When Heap found out Appelbaum would be appearing on the panel, he tweeted to his followers that his plans had changed. That evening, he simply failed to turn up to an event where he was billed as the main attraction.

Other researchers who had attempted to contact Heap were similarly snubbed. Such reticence did not endear him to the rest of the computer science and activist community. After *Newsweek*'s uncritical hagiography last August, the opposition to Haystack began to snowball. John Graham-Cumming, a respected coder and author, called Haystack 'vaporware', damning geek slang for code that does not exist except as advertising copy. Graham-Cunning noted that Heap's CV was heavier on the marketing than the programming skills. 'I guess he might have a hidden crypto background,' he commented, 'but I'm also guessing he's no Phil Zimmerman.' Evgeny Morozov, the sceptical author of *The Net Delusion*, picked up the trail and was sniffing around Haystack as an example of US State Department naivete.

My last meeting with Heap was in the middle of all this in the first week of September 2010. Once again, he wouldn't meet in an office, so this time we sat in a crowded cafe. He was far more open than I'd ever seen him before. He showed me what he said was Haystack working on his laptop. He explained that Haystack was only being used by a small circle of trusted experts. He confessed to me that what money Haystack had ever collected had almost gone, spent on servers that only a few test users had ever accessed. He even came very close to agreeing that an independent computer security researcher, also present, could audit the code. Most importantly, he told me I could tell others what I had seen.

Then Heap paused, and placed a condition on my reporting. If I said anything, Heap told me, I should mention Daniel more, because Daniel was extremely irritated that he was constantly being written out of the Haystack story.

Wait. Who was Daniel?

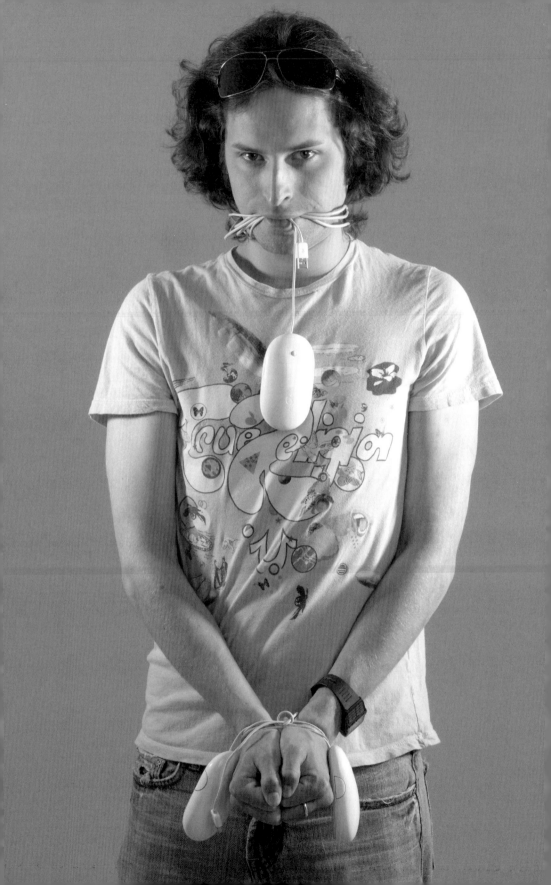

Daniel, it turned out, was Daniel Colascione. Colascione's involvement in Haystack wasn't a secret, exactly, but neither was it a highly publicised fact. He'd get an occasional mention in the sidelines of articles that were mostly about Heap. Heap said he always tried to get Daniel a credit. Then again, Heap had never mentioned Colascione to me before.

Which is strange, because it was soon to transpire that Colascione was the actual mastermind behind the Haystack code.

When I posted my summary of Heap's conversation to the net, I got a call from Appelbaum. Just from the outline of how Haystack worked, he was worried. Was this really being used by activists in Iran? He listed off a bunch of potential security vulnerabilities he'd gleaned from my skeletal description of how Haystack worked. They didn't seem that serious, but I forwarded his comments to Heap nonetheless. On a whim, I cc'd them to what I deduced was Colascione's email address, and one of the lawyers who had assisted Heap in obtaining an export license.

An explosion of phone calls and emails followed. On a phone call with me, Heap said unhappily that he knew that something like this would happen if he ever opened up about Haystack. The lawyer demanded from me whether Appelbaum knew that the software was being tested, and that this was 'a dangerous game'.

Finally, Colascione called me from Seattle. By comparison to Appelbaum, Heap, and the lawyer, he sounded calm, even resigned. He'd explain everything, he said.

The next day, Colascione uncloaked on an internet mailing list we both subscribed to, announcing to the world that he had written 'every line' of Haystack. He told us that he'd resigned from the project months earlier, out of disagreements over the project's operation. (So this was why Haystack appeared to be vaporware for so long). Now, he was agreeing to return, because Heap had agreed to run the project more openly. He described Haystack's internal structure in more detail than Heap ever did, or perhaps could.

Heap's behaviour began to make much more sense. His secret wasn't that he was a conman: he was a spokesman. Heap had avoided talking to technical people, because he wasn't the technical expert. The media had wanted to create a single super-genius and Heap had gone along with it. He was fine talking to politicians, bureaucrats and the media, but the moment anyone who knew anything about Haystack started asking him the tough questions, the front would collapse.

Appelbaum posted to the same list, saying that he had spoken to Heap, and Heap had agreed to shut down Haystack's central servers until the

Austin Heap after he won the Guardian's MediaInnovation award, March 2010
Credit: Andy Hall/Guardian News & Media Ltd 2010

81

problems could be addressed. Experts began to suggest improvements and fixes, and welcomed Colascione as a talented fellow coder. The age of secrecy for Haystack, it seemed, was over.

The tough questions were only just beginning, however. And it turned out there were some secrets about Haystack that even Colascione was not privy to.

When Appelbaum called me the next evening, I was on the Caltrain, the double-decker commuter train that ferries geeks up and down the backbone of Silicon Valley. He spoke rapidly, barely containing his anger. 'Do you have a publicly accessible webserver?' he said. 'Log into it now.'

Balancing my laptop and my mobile, switched to speakerphone, on my lap in the corner of a seat, I tapped into a command line window, and watched as Appelbaum accessed my webserver, using the Haystack software I had seen Heap demo a few days previously.

Somehow, Jake had got hold of the supposedly tightly controlled test client that Heap had shown me in the cafe. And now he was using it just as Haystack was meant to be used, as an encrypted, disguised funnel for data, despite Heap's claim that he had shut the service down.

Once he had got hold of what Austin had described to me as the Haystack test client, Appelbaum and his colleagues had set to work examining the whole of the Haystack system. They had found indications there that the Haystack code was more than just structurally suspect. It was doing a bunch of things that no anti-censorship software used by at-risk activists should do. And Appelbaum, acting as an attacker like the Iranian government might, was learning information about the potential users of Haystack that no third-party interceptor should ever have been able to find out.

I made some technical checks myself, then called Heap, and said what Appelbaum had told me. At first he denied that the server was still running. Then when I explained what I had seen, he denied that Appelbaum could possibly have got hold of a copy of the client program.

I knew that Heap and Colascione had both described Haystack as in a testing phase. But who was testing it? How many people had this software? Heap had reassured me that it was 'less than 50', and that its distribution was tightly controlled. But clearly Heap had lost control of that distribution. He even seemed to have lost control of his ability to shut the service down.

Then as I went into more detail, he patched Colascione into the call.

I repeated what Appelbaum had told me to the two of them. I told him one of the secrets Appelbaum had uncovered from his analysis. 'No, no,' said Colascione, more worried than I had heard him before, 'there's no way anyone could discover that.'

'Actually Dan,' said Heap, to the only other person in the world who understood Haystack's secrets, 'there is.'

As Heap and Colascione began to talk together about secrets that had been kept, and secrets that had been lost, I hung up.

Here's the final frustration for me. I spent the last two years meeting Heap in bars and cafes, slowly trying to persuade him to open up, and share some of Haystack's secrets to the world, or at least to some friendly experts. But I can't tell you what I learned on that train without potentially endangering whoever might have used the Haystack test software seriously. Applebaum doesn't think it's safe. I've never been able to get an assurance from Colascione that it would be okay to tell a wider public. He, understandably, thinks that it's better to let the whole thing go, and move on. I'm forced to self-censor what I know about this anti-censorship tool.

There's a principle of openness in secure communications design that dates back to the very beginnings of modern cryptography, a science and craft that devises truths so powerful the American government classed them as a munition, and that lets subversive voices in Iran and China battle dictators and beat billion-dollar censorship. It was coined by Auguste Kerckhoffs, a Dutch cryptographer in 1883.

Kerckhoffs' principle states that a cipher 'must not be required to be secret, and it must be able to fall into the hands of the enemy without inconvenience'.

Any security system depends on keeping some matters confidential. Strong cryptography requires a few hundred bits of a 'private key'. The most open software in the world might still want you to create a password to protect it. But a system that relies on too many secrets collapses when they inevitably leak out. With not much more than a program that Heap had uploaded to a few Iranians, Appelbaum had unravelled almost every element of how the Haystack test client worked. Anyone else who obtained those secrets can potentially hurt anyone who used the same Haystack code, or ever used it. Now we, too, were the reluctant keepers of those secrets.

Colascione resigned the next day, protesting mainly the continuing disorganisation of Heap's project, but adding of the code Appelbaum had analysed, 'it is as bad as [he] makes it out to be'. Heap shut down the Haystack server, for real.

Appelbaum and I told people to avoid Haystack, but we told them we couldn't tell them why. Many people didn't believe us, even when Haystack's lead – indeed, only programmer – agreed with the prognosis. What could we say? The sceptical were right to disbelieve. We were behaving exactly like Heap had done on that first meeting: closed, paranoid, unrevealing. Why trust a man who tells you to simply accept he has secrets to keep?

Since the last days of Haystack, my fears of the damage the software may have caused have decreased. Like epidemiologists tracking an outbreak, Colascione and others worked together to track who had received the software, and how far it had spread in the wild. As far as we can tell, it did not spread far. In the wave of Haystack's collapse, no one was arrested, and no one died.

Colascione himself has elaborated on the lessons from Haystack, and more, and come up with many new technical ideas that are being considered by others in anti-censorship systems. I'd say he's regarded as one of the promising new faces in open source circumvention systems.

In March 2010, the US government finally created a blanket export license for 'certain services and software incident to the exchange of personal communications over the internet, such as instant messaging, chat and email, social networking, sharing of photos and movies, web browsing, and blogging, provided that such services are publicly available at no cost to the user'. Even if Haystack will never be deployed, perhaps Heap and his lawyers' determined lobbying of the State Department may well have accelerated what should have been done years ago.

I've not spoken to Austin since my last phone call with him and Colascione. Like thousands of others, I do read his Twitter stream. He's still passionate about the Iranian Green movement, and has worked to spread news, videos and their work from within Iran across the net. If he's privately devastated by the collapse of the project that drove him into thousands of press articles, I don't see it in what he tweets to his public. If I had to guess, I'd say that he's relieved to no longer have to pretend to be the super-genius hacker, and happier to work in the background, doing the little things that smart technical people around the world do every day to promote free expression. A mirrored site here, a proxy server run there: you don't have to be a 'computer savant' to contribute to internet freedom.

I thought of asking him what he's up to for this article, but I didn't. It doesn't matter. Even if the story of Haystack seems to revolve around Heap, the real lesson is how little personalities should matter. The questions we should ask are how can we build tools that don't depend on secrets, or secret-keepers, publicists and publicity. And why should any-one need to know what one geek is doing right now? A man has a right to some secrets.

Appelbaum should be so lucky. As well as work on Tor, and reverse-engineering the secret flaws of Haystack, he also volunteers for WikiLeaks. Beginning in July 2010, for unstated reasons, he has been regularly detained on re-entering the United States by US customs agents. His mobile phones were seized, his laptop inspected, and paperwork in his luggage copied. In January of this year, the US Department of Justice obtained a sealed court order requiring Twitter to provide data, including addresses and bank account details, connected with five individuals con-nected to WikiLeaks, including Appelbaum. Twitter's lawyers successfully petitioned to unseal the order, and Appelbaum himself is challenging the subpoena.

Sometimes, you tell your secrets to the people in Washington, DC. Sometimes they come after yours. ❐

©Danny O'Brien
40(1): 73/85
DOI: 10.1177/0306422011400800
www.indexoncensorship.org

Danny O'Brien was the Electronic Frontier Foundation's international activist from 2007-2010, and is a founder of the UK's digital civil liberties organisation, the Open Rights Group. He now works as the internet advocacy coordinator at the Committee to Protect Journalists https://cpj.org/internet

ageni

спецслужбы под кон

АГЕНТУ?

досье   таймлайн   инфраструктура

Исследовательский центр Agentura.Ru борьба

...руктура ФСБ: Центральный аппарат

"...тура" Федеральной службы безопасности в результате реализац...

...ент внес изменения в Указ от 11.08.03 № 960 "Вопросы Федерал...

...рвого заместителя директора ФСБ, одного первого замести...

...ий директора ФСБ, в том числе одного статс-секретаря - замести...

— Александр Васильевич Бортников

...аместитель - Сергей Смирнов, председатель Совета РАТ...

...меститель директора - Владимир Егорович Про...

...й директора - Владимир Кулишов П...

...ического комитета (НА...

...ректора, стат...

OPEN SECRETS

The workings of the Russian secret services are now available online in unprecedented detail. **Andrei Soldatov** and **Irina Borogan** report

In 2000, we founded the website agentura.ru to publish information on the Russian secret services. In such a closed society as Russia, the only material available on the Federal Security Service (FSB) was fragmented: some official interviews in pro-Kremlin newspapers, short reports on special operations in the North Caucasus or verdicts on spy trials reported by wire agencies and dailies. At best, newspapers were able to publish investigations of particular shortcomings and scandals. Over the past ten years, the internet has transformed the landscape for monitoring the FSB, making it possible to construct a general picture of its activities. With the technology available to collect, systemise and present information, no matter where it was reported, it became possible for us to provide an insight into the workings of the secret services: the challenges they face and their relationship with the state.

By the summer of 2000, it was clear that the role of the Russian secret services was changing. Vladimir Putin, a KGB officer in the 80s and FSB director in the 90s, had been elected president, the scientific community had been shocked by spy trials against researchers initiated by the FSB and the second Chechen war had begun. In December 1999, Nikolai Patrushev succeeded

Vladimir Putin as director of the FSB and described his staff as 'the new nobility of Russia'. At the same time, the FSB remained almost completely impenetrable to public scrutiny. It enjoyed a combination of law enforcement and secret service functions, having the right to arrest people, carry out special operations, spy, conduct investigations and maintain its own detention facilities.

The biggest task for us was to create and maintain an updated guide to the structure of the Russian secret services. The aim was to list every department, division or branch of the FSB, and then to build up a profile, adding new information and using research from available archives. Every line in our guide to the secret services' structure (including the names of the heads of department) links to a source, which also protects us from prosecution. The FSB has always claimed that all information about its activities should be kept secret, including the identity of those personally responsible for operations. Journalists are not allowed to publish information about the personnel or structure of the secret services, so it was important for us to show that the names of the officers were already available in open sources.

The FSB was keen to keep its secrets away from the public

We modelled our website on Steven Aftergood's project on government secrecy at the Federation of American Scientists (www.fas.org), which works to promote public access to government information and to illuminate the apparatus of state secrecy. It publishes previously undisclosed or inaccessible government documents of public policy interest, as well as resources on intelligence policy. At the same time, as journalists rather than academics, we wanted to create a tool for gathering information for our own investigations.

From the beginning, we understood that agentura.ru (the name means community of agents, and ru is the country code for Russia) could not exploit the approach used by Steven Aftergood, based on open source research and supplemented by Freedom of Information requests. In Russia, there was no Freedom of Information Act until January 2010, while journalists' and historians' requests for information to be declassified are rarely successful. The FSB remained in charge of its archives and records, and was keen to keep its secrets away from the public.

The only possible approach for us was to read through published material and look for disregarded, but significant, information. Nikita Petrov, the deputy head of the Memorial Center and an expert on the history of Soviet terror, had used the same method when he initially became interested in the Soviet security services' history in the 70s. 'Back in the Soviet era, even as early as the 20s, information about departmental heads and their deputies was all published in local papers,' he told us. 'Under Stalin, fulsome information was printed regarding awards given to those serving with the security services. It was all out in the open, there were names, titles, full names, not just initials.' This Soviet tradition remains mostly unchanged, especially in the regions: newspapers continue to give editorial space to the heads of local FSB departments.

Furthermore, press coverage of the secret services' activities has changed fundamentally since the fall of the Soviet Union. The quantity and quality of reporting in the Russian press improved in the 90s, not only in Moscow-based papers, but in the new independent regional media. Both widely covered corruption scandals involving the secret services.

Journalists in the regions therefore became a particularly important source for us. The FSB is comprised of two unequal parts: its headquarters, which has never had a staff of more than a few thousand personnel, and its regional offices, estimated to employ hundreds of thousands of individuals. The impact of the reporting activities of regional branches therefore far exceeds its immediate reach. Provincial state security branches are constantly shaping the secret services from within, due to a system of personnel rotation: colonels and generals are moved from one regional directorate to another and are eventually offered positions on the central staff at FSB headquarters. As a result, information about regional career paths can shed light on the processes inside the security services. It's well known, for example, that the leadership of the FSB is packed with officers from the St Petersburg branch, including the three most recent FSB directors – Vladimir Putin (1998–9), Nikolai Patrushev (1999–2008) and Alexander Bortnikov (2008–).

Events in the regions can also illuminate new trends in national security policy. For example, in 1997 the FSB tried to prosecute military journalist Grigory Pasko in Vladivostok, the far east of Russia. Pasko was accused of espionage in a case supervised by German Ugryumov, then head of the local FSB department. He was found guilty and sentenced to four years in jail in December 2001. Ugryumov was promoted to deputy director of the FSB in Moscow and put in charge of counter-terrorism operations in Chechnya in January 2001. It was widely rumoured that he was slated to become the next director of the FSB before his death in May 2001. Lower-ranking officers on the Pasko case were also promoted. Investigator Alexander Yegorkin, who headed the investigation, was moved to Moscow, where he led the military counter-intelligence division at the FSB investigative directorate. Further spy scandals in the early noughties, initiated by the FSB in Perm and Nizhny Novgorod, indicate that they were becoming a popular method for furthering the careers of regional officers.

From the beginning, we chose to work closely with the print media, always publishing our stories in newspapers first, to protect ourselves from government intimidation. All our investigations were checked according to traditional journalistic standards and by the lawyers of the respective papers, and attempts to discredit our reports failed. The FSB initially put pressure on us following our coverage of the Nord-Ost hostage taking in October 2002: they tried to accuse us of divulging state secrets and raided the offices of the newspaper *Versiya*. Their tactics were widely covered in the Russian and international media, and Freimut Duve, the OSCE Representative on Freedom of the Media, issued a special statement of concern. The same approach was repeated in 2007 when the FSB this time paid a visit to the offices of *Novaya Gazeta* following our report on the secret services' investigations in spy cases. This, in turn, helped us to resist attempts to stop our reporting.

Hackers replaced the main page with the picture of a bear

The internet has also posed some unexpected ethical problems. In the mid-noughties, we launched a forum at agentura.ru to provide a space for public discussion. Rival factions in the secret services, mostly in the regions, began to use it to disseminate information. The most notorious example was in Vladivostok. In the late noughties, the city witnessed a fierce struggle between the local FSB branch and the customs service, reportedly over control of smuggling from China. A general in the customs service was sent to jail and accused the FSB of prosecuting him because of his revelations about corruption. Rival factions posted scanned copies of FSB documents and customs reports on the forum of agentura.ru and then had them republished in local papers, with agentura.ru cited as the source. We had no resources to investigate the story ourselves or to check the authenticity of the documents, and it was rather disturbing to see the website turned into a battlefield. Eventually we decided to stop the documents from being published on the forum.

Last April, agentura.ru was attacked by hackers – a combination of distributed denial of service attacks (DDoS) and trojan viruses – along with some liberal media websites. It is possible that we were the victim of the so-called 'hacker patriots', nationalists who carry out cyberattacks on the websites of enemies of the state, a list that ranges from Chechen sites abroad to the liberal media at home. The series of attacks almost ruined the website: security was breached and the main page was replaced by hackers with a picture of a bear. As a result, last summer we were forced to arrange for the website to be hosted in the US. This kind of pressure has turned out to be the most difficult to resist: the sophisticated web-security technologies are costly and it's almost impossible to find out the source of the attacks.

Agentura.ru now has a profile of every branch of the FSB. In at least one case, we managed to convince the security services themselves to provide information, by insisting that otherwise we would publish what we found on the internet. Sources, however, are drying up: insiders are becoming increasingly unwilling to talk to journalists, partly because the Kremlin no longer even bothers to respond to investigations. In 2005–6, the Kremlin also changed the rules for covering counter-terrorism operations, effectively preventing journalists from travelling to the areas of operations, including the North Caucasus, and obtaining independent information. As a result, many journalists who covered the secret services in the 90s have abandoned the subject. At the same time, Moscow's newspapers are cutting back on investigative journalism, because of the expense and the danger. In the wake of these changes, agentura.ru has now grown into a mini think-tank, and remains the first and the only independent website on the secret services in Russia. Not only have journalists begun asking us to provide comment and expert assessments, but even the FSB itself: in 2006, we were very surprised when the Federal Security Service branch in the republic of Tuva sent an email asking us to forward them everything we had on the Mongolian special services. We chose not to answer. ❐

© Andrei Soldatov and Irina Borogan
40(1): 86/91
DOI: 10.1177/0306422011399698
www.indexoncensorship.org

Andrei Soldatov and **Irina Borogan** are the authors of *The New Nobility: The Restoration of Russia's Security State and the Enduring Legacy of the KGB* (Public Affairs)

The defining work from one of China's most banned writers

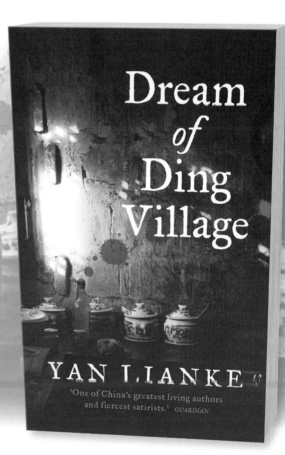

'One of China's greatest living authors and fiercest satirists.'
Jonathan Watts, *Guardian*

In *The Dream of Ding Village*, Yan Lianke takes as his subject the contemporary AIDS blood-contamination scandal in Henan province, where villagers were coerced into selling large amounts of blood and then infected with the HIV virus as they were injected with plasma to prevent anaemia. *The Dream of Ding Village* focuses on one such village, and the story of one family torn apart, to trace the life and death of an entire community.

21st April 2011   £12.99   Paperback

Published by corsair
An imprint of Constable & Robinson

GOING LOCAL

If the US's internet freedom agenda is going to be effective, it must start by supporting grassroots activists on their own terms, says **Ivan Sigal**

In January, the US State Department issued a tender for $30m in funding for US non-profit organisations to support internet freedom. It was the first major injection of cash since Secretary of State Hillary Clinton announced the government's commitment more than a year ago. 'On their own, new technologies do not take sides in the struggle for freedom and progress,' she declared. 'But the United States does. We stand for a single internet where all of humanity has equal access to knowledge and ideas.'

In theory, this sounds like just the sort of thing that the US government should be supporting: universal access to a single, open internet that allows everyone in the world to receive and share information equally is a notion that fits with the aims of Article 19 of the Universal Declaration of Human Rights, which privileges the rights of individuals to speak and receive information irrespective of their citizenship. It also highlights the potential of the internet's networked design, which favours equal access to users. However, the internet freedom mantra is too often articulated as a technological solution for problems that are actually political, social, legal and economic. Online activism is seen as a structural fix, as a simple solution for complex, multi-faceted dilemmas. It is an approach that misses out on real concerns and local contexts, contests for power and substantive clashes over how to govern.

Local activists using online tools to organise or share information in many countries fear that their work will be compromised by the US government's focus on digital media. If the State Department cares so much about the effect of the internet on information control, the argument runs, then foreign governments might perceive that it is being used to threaten their stability.

My colleague Sami Ben Gharbia, the advocacy director for Global Voices, has been one of the most articulate critics of American policy and its impact, in a long essay published last year on his blog outlining the risks for Arab activists. He argues passionately for independent, homegrown initiatives and describes the US's agenda as 'extremely dangerous for the digital activism grassroots movement' and a cover for strategic geopolitics: 'Foreign money delegitimises political and social activism. And once delegitimised, activism cannot influence social and political changes and cannot be supported by the rest of the society.'

By this, Ben Gharbia means grassroots activism that depends on local support and represents local interests. His perspective privileges volunteer, citizen efforts over professional activism. Activists who remain volunteers, rather than depend upon their activism for their income, cannot be accused of profiting from their ideals. The long-term consequence of an activist approach that remains steadfastly civic and volunteer might be a political system more open to citizen participation, rather than politicians who benefit from perpetuating power. At such times, activists may find themselves in a position to join in the process of governing, rather than stand outside it. A recent example is the invitation to blogger and activist Slim Amamou to join the Tunisian interim government; similar cases of bloggers coming to politics have occurred in recent years in the Philippines and Malaysia.

The State Department's approach has until recently explicitly favoured a bias towards increasing access to international information sources from the West over the creation of information, networking and local activism. This bias has primarily taken the form of support for increased use and promotion of circumvention technology. It has also neglected other kinds of threats to online expression that are the greatest concern for many local activists: from distributed denial of service attacks (DDoS), hacking of websites, licensing and other regulatory restrictions, to physical attacks and arrests.

Acting president Fouad Mbazaa greets blogger Slim Amamou, briefly
Tunisia's new secretary of state in charge of sports, Tunis, 18 January 2011
Credit: Fethi Belaid/AFP/Getty

This agenda has been substantially driven by members of Congress, who want to take a more aggressive approach toward China and Iran. They seek to influence US foreign policy and have earmarked $50m for circumvention technology since 2007 to do so. Allied lobbyists have also conducted a concerted advocacy campaign in major publications to support this position.

In its January tender, the State Department has expanded its focus beyond circumvention technologies to support local online content providers and digital activists. It now also seeks to support technology projects that provide secure mobile communications, digital safety training, technology skills for digital activists, protection and support of local content, emergency funds, public policy initiatives, and research and monitoring components. The initiative explicitly names regions and countries that practice censorship and filtering, as well as other forms of speech repression: 'East Asia, including China and Burma; the Near East, including Iran; Southeast Asia;

the South Caucasus; Eurasia, including Russia; Central Asia; Latin America, including Cuba and Venezuela; and Africa.' The shift is likely to have been influenced by criticisms from academic and activist communities of the State Department's approach: privileging access to external information over support for internal activism and local agendas.

Despite the support for different tactics, the question of whether net freedom remains an instrument for other foreign policy agendas is still open. While the US government may support the principle of universal and equitable internet access, the recent practice of the State Department has in fact been to subordinate it to broader foreign policy priorities, balancing support for freedom and democracy with competing economic and security interests. This tension illuminates a gap between the language of internet freedom and the actual behaviour of the US government, its policy priorities and its complex and sometimes cosy relationships with numerous authoritarian regimes.

Amongst the countries that are the worst offenders in internet censorship – in terms of filtering and regulation as well as rights restrictions on speech, association, and political activity – several states receive economic and security assistance from the US that dwarfs any support for internet freedom. The potential effects of this policy split can be seen in the case of Ali Abdulemam, a well-known Bahraini blogger who co-founded the online news portal BahrainOnline.org. Abdulemam was arrested as part of a wider crackdown on civic activism in the second half of 2010. Regardless, the US is planning to sell Bahrain $70m in arms, and its neighbour Saudi Arabia, with a similar record of internet censorship, is planning a purchase of $60bn.

The commentator Rami Khouri has succinctly observed that 'feeding both the jailer and the prisoner is not a sustainable or sensible policy'. From a policy perspective, of course, supporting both the jailer and the prisoner might have a logic when combined with quiet pressure for reform. It is a long-practiced diplomatic strategy to use a combination of cooperation and pressure on rights issues. The consequences of such policies, however, create systematic uncertainty and mistrust from the perspective of rights advocates. They are acutely aware that their agendas will usually receive only qualified support, and that support might shift or vanish in the face of other policy priorities.

In the world of online activism, many individuals and movements are particularly sensitive to how they represent their work publicly, with whom they choose to align themselves, and whether or not associations with governments, whether domestic or foreign, as well as other advocates, hurt or help their goals.

Local rights advocates seek engagement from external actors that is sensitive to their context and agenda. This is true whether they resent the appropriation of their issues for other agendas, or more simply want to determine what kind of representation helps their particular causes. External funding that brings a different set of priorities threatens this autonomy.

The State Department's policy is also handicapped by focusing solely overseas and ignoring the increase in internet control, intermediary liability and threats to anonymity and privacy domestically, and in democratic countries. When western countries such as Australia and Italy seek to create policies that require internet intermediaries such as search engines to be responsible for their content, it is hypocritical for the West to complain about similar practices in China. When the FBI promotes a requirement for telecommunications and internet providers to create back doors to encrypted internet and cell phone data, it's hard to complain about authoritarian surveillance. When security advocates in the United States seek to decrease online anonymity and privacy, it's hard to argue for the protection of those same rights for activists in other countries.

Other aspects of US foreign policy also impinge on internet freedom, in particular US Treasury and Commerce restrictions on tech companies making their products available in countries such as Iran, Syria or North Korea. The consequences of these policies mean that many online tools and websites most useful for activists, but owned by American companies, are simply not available.

While governments will work to harmonise their various interests, it is unlikely that tension between rights advocacy and economic and security concerns will vanish. The US government is not likely to jeopardise its energy supply for the benefit of increased freedoms for Saudi citizens, for instance, even if some State Department officials would prefer a different approach. The government's caution around encouraging President Mubarak to resign in the face of mass popular protests against his regime is another example. States with nuclear strike capacities will always receive more attention than those without – this is one reason Pakistan, North Korea and Israel pursued nuclear technology so assiduously.

How, then, to engage the US and other governments in a constructive debate over how funds are used, to minimise damage and possibly to do some good?

The paradox for grassroots activists is that at present only governments have the capacity to make and enforce rules, and support the industrial infrastructures that underpin the internet and the legal and regulatory frameworks that give us our rights. While there is a vigorous movement to support global mechanisms to govern the internet, at present they still rely on the goodwill and support of governments. The goal for many activists is good government, fairness and transparency, enforcement of our fundamental freedoms, and a vigorous and open debate over the limits of those freedoms at the margins.

The extraordinary story of Tunisia this year, as well as protests across the Middle East and North Africa, are examples of this dilemma. The fall of the Ben Ali government was facilitated by information technology rather than caused by it. However the channels of information people used to organise, protest and share information culminated in a successful campaign for freedom of expression and the end of a censorship regime.

For activists, the real challenge now lies ahead: how to shift from a position of steadfast opposition to constructive engagement? How to ensure that their revolution doesn't go the way of, say, the Kyrgyz Republic's Tulip Revolution in 2003, which held the promise of democratic reform, but was captured by ethnic and economic interest groups, and was eventually also overthrown.

Some activists, such as blogger Slim Amamou, chose to briefly join a unified reform government – an amazing turn after being arrested at the height of the protests. Other activists involved in the Tunisian online portal nawaat.org, such as Sami Ben Gharbia, will retain a watchdog role, but try to ramp up the technology skills and local networks of activists, to ensure and maintain openness and political participation over the long term.

As for foreign government support, the Tunisian case is a chance to get things right. The best way to do this is to start by listening, and being sensitive to local concerns about privacy, insecurity and the extremely contested dynamics of local politics. Tunisians have been grappling with the question of how to form a unity government, how to hold elections, who to admit into the political process and the actual process of governing after the elections.

From the perspective of information access and media technology, the most important thing that outsiders can now do is to voice support for an environment of open and vigorous debate, run by Tunisians, in their own space. Funding for direct online activism, content production, or the sponsoring of platforms might be seen as intrusive. Support for educational initiatives, infrastructure and access, and efforts to support and nurture public, civic spaces of all kinds is a more appropriate engagement over the long term. The same obtains for engagement with the civic spaces of other authoritarian regimes. The US should not remain stuck in the Cold

War imagery of falling walls and curtains, and it should instead emphasise local and national empowerment, dialogue and debate. It should privilege support for local, incremental change, avoiding big ideological statements in favour of attentive and specific responses to particular challenges. In this way, many organisations and activists have quietly been using technology in the past decade, with a lower profile and a focus on security and privacy.

For activists, encouraging governments to change their behaviour entails a variety of tactics. Now, as before the advent of internet advocacy, this means everything from engagement to monitoring, from working internally to public statements and critiques. No one tactic is right for every occasion. Rather, the tactic needs to fit the goal, and choices around the level of risk, public profile, anonymity and engagement made accordingly.

For all governments, the fact of a networked, global information space makes contradictions between word and deed in policy more easily evident. Congruence is a key element in trust, and this is where many foreign policy challenges lie. For instance, the challenge of Pakistani or Yemini perceptions of US motives suffers from a persistent failure to accord non-US citizens the same value as American citizens, as is evidenced by ongoing drone strikes that also hit innocents.

This is a direct contradiction to a stated policy goal of affording everyone in the world the same rights. The subordination of a rights agenda to economic and security concerns demonstrates that the US has not yet met its rhetoric with commensurate policy responses. A foreign policy that seeks congruence on this subject would look very different, perhaps more humane, but with a different set of challenges. ❐

©Ivan Sigal
40(1): 93/99
DOI: 10.1177/0306422011400799
www.indexoncensorship.org

Ivan Sigal is the executive director of Global Voices (http://globalvoicesonline.org), a non-profit online global citizens' media initiative. He was previously a senior fellow at the US Institute of Peace and regional director for Internews Network covering Asia, Central Asia and Afghanistan

SURVIVING LUKASHENKO

To work as a journalist in Belarus takes courage and ingenuity. **James Kirchick** looks at the climate for alternative media in the aftermath of the elections

Visiting Minsk in the days before Belarus's December presidential election, one would not have recognised a country whose claim to infamy is the moniker of 'last dictatorship in Europe'. With prodding from the European Union, President Alexander Lukashenko lifted many of the onerous restrictions that had previously existed on opposition political campaigning, with nine candidates ultimately qualifying for the ballot. Live presidential debates were broadcast on state television and radio (though Lukashenko himself declined to participate). Challengers were allowed to hold public events (provided that they gave the authorities two days' notice) and were given free airtime on state-controlled media, which many of them used to lodge specific complaints against the government. Though lacking the uninhibited, 24/7 onslaught of information that's become all too familiar in western democracies, the campaign nonetheless featured many of the atmospherics recognisable to observers of the small-town, local politicking of America or Britain.

But in the end, the apparently pluralistic qualities of the Belarusian presidential campaign were just that: atmospherics. The hopes that Lukashenko had finally decided upon a path to liberal reform, and that the EU's carrot-and-stick approach had borne fruit, came crashing down on 19 December when Belarusian riot police descended upon a crowd of peaceful demonstrators protesting evident election fraud. Within minutes of polls officially closing, the government announced that Lukashenko had won nearly 80 per cent of the vote on the preposterously high figure of 90 per cent turnout. Nearly 700 people were arrested, including the leading opposition candidates. The US and EU have since imposed sanctions.

Despite the outward appearance of an open campaign, the Lukashenko regime has effectively rendered political opposition moot through its near domination of the press. It has silenced critical voices through two means: state control of mass media outlets like television and radio, and onerous registration laws that make the practice of independent journalism a dangerous pursuit.

Most Belarusians get their news through television, which is entirely controlled by the state. In the run-up to the election, the Organisation for Security and Cooperation in Europe found that 89 per cent of 'political and election-related news' on television was devoted to Lukashenko, the 'tone' of which 'was exclusively positive or neutral, while the tone of coverage of the other candidates was mostly negative and in some cases neutral'. One knowledgeable observer of the Belarusian political scene told me that state television regularly portrays regime critics as 'thieves, tax cheats, and ham-handed'. ('I watch it just to laugh,' a Belarusian friend says). This is all a conscious echo of Lukashenko's crudely expressed attitudes about the opposition; his repertoire alternates between vicious threats and feigned indifference. 'I don't have dialogue with bandits and subversives,' he replied when asked if he would meet with his opponents following the election. As to the protests that were being planned in Minsk on the evening of the 19th, he predicted: 'There will be nobody at the square today.'

The government controls the country's printing presses and means of distribution, enabling it to regulate the print media. In addition to four state-funded newspapers, two private ones (the weekly *Nasha Niva* and the twice-weekly *Narodnaya Volia*) are allowed to publish, but they have miniscule circulations: *Narodnaya Volia* distributes 23,000 copies and *Nasha Niva* 6,500. Given these challenges, many Belarusians looking for unfiltered news have to turn to foreign broadcasting outlets like Radio Free Europe/Radio Liberty's Belarusian-language service or the Polish-sponsored Belsat television (which Lukashenko has characteristically described as a 'stupid and uncongenial project').

*A protester arrested during post-election demonstrations gestures
from his prison cell at a detention centre in Minsk, 29 December 2010
Credit: Vasily Fedosenko/Reuters*

Belarusians, especially young people, are increasingly turning to the internet for news. In addition to forcing internet service providers to collect information on their users, the government routinely blocks opposition and independent news websites, all in an effort to control what Lukashenko has termed 'anarchy on the internet'. On 19 December, the regime shut down many of these sites, in addition to blocking Gmail and Twitter. In the aftermath of the protests, it began a vicious and extensive crackdown on independent journalists.

Iryna Vidanava has found a clever way around these barriers. The publisher of *34 Multimedia Magazine*, she has married the concept of samizdat – underground publications circulated by dissidents behind the Iron Curtain – with new media, distributing her publication on compact discs. *34* is the latter-day incarnation of a Belarusian-language magazine founded by university students in 1924 called *Student Thought*. The magazine was revived in the 80s under the same name and later taken over by Vidanava in 1998. Her father is a prominent opposition journalist and author of a book about Stalin-era repression. She officially registered the publication at the time, and began to cover topics that the state media wouldn't touch, like university corruption.

In December 2003, the authorities shut the magazine down, just as it was beginning to turn a profit. Vidanava continued publishing, however, distributing it in small batches at select locations and via email. In November 2005, plainclothes officers from the KGB (one of the most unsubtle touches of Lukashenko's regime is the decision to maintain the Soviet-era name of the country's internal intelligence service) raided her office and confiscated the print run. The following January, she decided to distribute the magazine on cheap and easily copied compact discs, distributed at stores and clubs frequented by young people. 'With news, you have to be dynamic,' she told me in Minsk. 'You cannot wait three months to come out.' Vidanava also changed the name to *34*: the number of the article in the Belarusian consti-tution guaranteeing freedom of expression, and because the letters C and D are the third and fourth in the Latin alphabet. The magazine's website (http://34mag.net) was created in 2008, but the CD remains an important means of distribution.

Last summer, a law was passed requiring all Belarusian internet sys-tems, information resources and networks to register with the government. Internet cafes have to record users' personal data and the websites they visit, while Belarusian news sites are required to move to the Belarusian '.by' domain, putting them under the jurisdiction of the state. 'While the conse-quences are not yet clear,' Vidanava writes, 'there is little doubt that the decree will be used to control and suppress independent online resources. It will also strengthen self-censorship.' As one of the more outspoken sectors of society, youth media like *34* may be particularly vulnerable to the authorities. Given this bleak picture, Vidanava believes that it is 'important to maintain as many channels of independent information as possible'.

Much of *34's* content is, however, apolitical. A recent issue entitled 'Take a Look at Yourself!' features a series of video interviews with young Belarusians on the wide boulevards of Minsk. Over a score of techno music, they discuss what superpowers they would like to possess and recommend hangover cures. A sense of optimism prevails: the interview subjects smile and laugh, and there is hardly any sense of the despair that has gripped the country in the wake of the December events and ongoing crackdown. Vidanava takes the former eastern bloc dissidents as her inspiration and is clearly a product of this intellectual heritage. She is part of what she describes as 'the creative opposition', which, like its European forebears, is inspired by 'alternative culture to take up alternative politics, paving the way for political change'.

When the magazine does address politics, it tries not to sermonise. Vidanava explains that this approach is necessary not only to evade the watchful eyes of the regime, but more importantly to strike a chord with a young audience understandably cynical about politics. This is a country, remember, where courses on 'state ideology' are mandatory in university. The Lukashenko regime tries to control practically every aspect of youth life, 'because it fears any free ideas, whether homegrown or from the West', Vidanava writes. A recent *34* feature profiled the careers of ex-politicians, contrasting the charitable work of Bill Clinton to the post-political life of Alberto Fujimori, currently serving a sentence of more than 30 years in prison for a variety of human rights abuses he committed as president of Peru. The message, Vidanava says, is that a leader can leave politics and still have a productive life. One doesn't have to be an expert political analyst to understand which leader she was attempting to mock.

While *34* and the oppositional culture that it exemplifies have provided a refreshing tonic to a stultifying and increasingly repressive regime, there is a limit to how much change it can actually effect. 'Many young people, frustrated by the inability of the opposition to mount a challenge to the country's tough ruler, are beginning to wonder why they should even bother with poorly attended town halls, rigged elections, exorbitant fines, and inevitable jail time if the internet allows doing politics remotely, anonymously, and on the cheap,' writes Evgeny Morozov, the Belarusian-born social media expert. 'But this has proved no more than utopian dreaming: no angry tweets or text messages, no matter how eloquent, have been able to rekindle the democratic spirit of the masses, who, to a large extent, have drowned in a bottomless reservoir of spin and hedonism, created by a government that has read Huxley.'

From his bullying rhetoric right down to his ogre-like physical demeanour, Lukashenko – a former collective farmer – plays the part of the humourless Soviet apparatchik with aplomb. Sporting a comb-over and moustache, he possesses a face whose default countenance is a scowl. The 'press conference' he delivered the day after the election violence could not have provided a more fitting contrast to the *joie de vivre* and inquisitiveness of *34*. Sitting behind a desk on a massive stage, Lukashenko addressed a vast auditorium full of applauding automatons, in a scene reminiscent of Soviet-era Communist

Party conclaves. There, he promised an end to 'senseless democracy', a spit in the face to the European officials who, just weeks before, were indulging him with promises of billions in aid if he would just hold one free and fair election. He denounced the 'banditry' and 'criminality' of his opponents. And as for the independent media, they would be responsible 'for every written word'. Following this harangue, a line of official 'journalists' lined up in the aisles behind microphones to ask questions as if they were attending a lecture.

I asked Vidanava what she considers to be the regime's worst offence. 'At the very philosophical level, I would say that it has made people stop being critical and think for themselves.' Not the beatings and arrests, the corruption and nepotism, nor the complete failure to modernise the economy and provide a future for her own generation of Belarusians. These sorts of abuses and blunders can, after all, be changed through accountable government and the right policies. But the damage Lukashenko has done and continues to do to this critical human faculty – independent thought – is something that will take generations to repair. For now, Vidanava and her readers will keep on asking questions. 'You can't completely bury this spirit,' she tells me. 'You can only suppress it.' ❏

©James Kirchick
40(1): 101/106
DOI: 10.1177/0306422011399691
www.indexoncensorship.org

James Kirchick is writer at large with Radio Free Europe/Radio Liberty based in Prague and a contributing editor to the *New Republic* in Washington

New from SAQI BOOKS

New collection of essays from the Middle East and International Relations expert, Fred Halliday

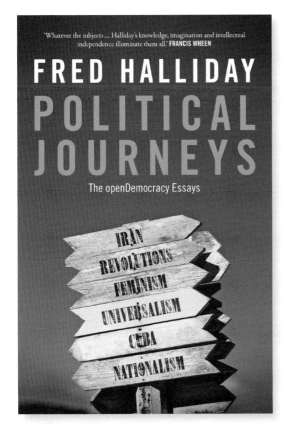

£14.99
March 2011
978-0-86356-461-1

Political Journeys
The openDemocracy Essays
Fred Halliday

'Unlike many veterans of 1968, Fred Halliday never stopped listening and observing and thinking in the present tense. There are fresh insights and shafts of enlightenment on every page of this invigorating collection of essays. Whatever the subjects – from Auschwitz to Armenia, Beirut to Barcelona – Halliday's knowledge, imagination and intellectual independence illuminate them all.'
Francis Wheen

'Fred Halliday's *Political Journeys* range over wide intellectual and political landscapes, with brilliant insights, absorbing narratives, lucid writing and subtle humour. The Middle East, the Cold War, Islamism, imperialism and international relations, the dilemmas of our time, are all illuminated with deep analyses coupled with passionate commitment to the universal values of justice and human rights.'
Sami Zubaida

www.saqibooks.com

EX
EX

A censorship chronicle incorporating technology stories from the *Age*, Agence France-Presse (AFP), allafrica.com, Al Jazeera, Amnesty International, Arabic Network for Human Rights Information (ANHRI), Ars Technica, asianews.it, Associated Press (AP), Bahrain Center for Human Rights, BBC, Bianet, Business Week, bizcommunity.com, businessweek.com, *Calgary Herald*, Center for Journalism in Extreme Situations (CJES), Channel 4, Chosun Ilbo, CNET News, CNN, Committee to Protect Journalists (CPJ), *Courier Mail*, cultofmac.com, Digital Journal, Digital Rights in Europe (EDRI), the *Enquirer*, Eurasia Review, First Amendment Coalition, *Guardian*, *Haaretz*, Huffington Post, Human Rights in China (HRIC), Human Rights Watch (HRW), *Independent*, InformationWeek.com, IPS Communication Foundation, *Irish Times*, *Jerusalem Post*, Knight Center, Media Foundation, Mizzima, *New Republic*, *New York Times*, Norwegian PEN, Radio Free Europe (RFE/RL), Radio France Internationale (RFI), Raidió Teilifís Éireann (RTE), Reuters, Reporters sans frontières (RSF), *Sunday Morning Herald*, Softpedia, Southeast Asian Press Alliance (SEAPA) *Sydney Morning Herald*, *Telegraph*, techcrunch.com, TeleGeography, *Times of India*, *Trinidad Guardian*, *Wall Street Journal*, *Washington Post*, *Wired*, Xinhua, *Daily Yomiuri*, *Zambia Post* and other organisations affiliated with the International Freedom of Expression Exchange (IFEX)

Australia

On 12 December 2010, Prime Minister Julia Gillard renewed her backing for an **internet filter** that will block access to a range of controversial content, including references to and images of rape, drug use, bestiality and child sex abuse. Google, Yahoo and Microsoft criticised the initiative, stating that it might set a precedent for further censorship. (RTE)

The Australian Commonwealth Games Association placed a ban on athletes using **social media** for the duration of the Commonwealth Games in Delhi, which took place in October 2010. Officials cited the threat of terrorism as the reason for the measure. (*Courier Mail*)

In July 2010, the government's privacy commissioner stated that Google had acted in violation of the country's privacy laws. An investigation was ordered in May after privacy advocates raised concerns that the company's **Street Map** service collected data via Wi-Fi networks without the knowledge of citizens. (*Guardian*)

After receiving a freedom of expression request about plans to monitor **internet traffic** on 15 June 2010, the attorney general's department legal officer provided heavily censored documents relating to these proposals on 22 July. The officer claimed that the release of further details would lead to 'premature unnecessary debate'. Internet service providers (ISPs) involved in discussions also refused to make information available, and some industry sources stated the legislation could mean that the browsing history of every Australian citizen would be recorded. The claim was denied by the attorney general's spokesperson. (*Age, Sunday Morning Herald*)

Plans for ISPs to block child pornography **websites** were disrupted on 13 July 2010 after one provider, Internode, voiced concerns that the blacklists would block legal websites as well. The three largest internet companies, accounting for 70 per cent of Australian citizens with internet access, had already signed up to the proposals. (*Sydney Morning Herald*)

Comedian **Catherine Deveny** was dismissed from her job as a columnist at the *Age* on 5 May 2010 following inappropriate comments

she posted on Twitter during the Logie television awards. (*Guardian*)

In February 2010, hackers attacked **government websites**, including that of the country's communication minister. The attack, coordinated by activist group Anonymous, was launched as a protest against proposed internet laws, including mandatory ISP filtering. (Enquirer, *Sydney Morning Herald*)

Azerbaijan

Blogger **Emin Milli** was released from prison on 19 November 2010, a day after fellow blogger **Adnan Hajizade** was released. The court ruled that the remaining 14 months of their sentences should be 'suspended'. The two bloggers were arrested in July 2009 on charges of hooliganism after they posted a satirical video online. The relatives of the two imprisoned bloggers had appealed to President Obama to push for their release during talks with Azerbaijani leader Ilham Aliyev on 24 September. Charges against the bloggers remain and campaigners called for them to be overturned. (Amnesty International, RSF)

Bahrain

Al Jazeera online reporter **Bilal Randeree** was among the many journalists refused entry into the country as unrest in the capital entered its third day on 17 February 2011. Those reporting on the protests suffered harassment and there was a marked disruption to online access, with internet providers reporting increase in website filtering. Several accounts on video-sharing website **Bambuser** were blocked. (AFP, *Guardian*, technolog.msnbc.msn)

Twenty-five Shia Muslim opposition activists went on trial on 28 October 2010. Among them was blogger **Ali Abdulemam**, founder of the Bahrain Online forum, who was arrested on 4 September; the site was also closed down. Abduleman was arrested for distributing 'fabricated and malicious news' about the country and attempting to 'subvert the kingdom's security and stability'. The defendants pleaded not guilty to charges of plotting to overthrow the Sunni-led government and supporting 'terror cells'. Bahrain Online was closed down in September. (BBC, the *New Republic*)

As part of the government's crackdown on websites and other forms of new media in the run up to elections, the site and social media pages of opposition leader **Abdul-Wahab Hussain** were blocked by the Information Affairs Authority in October 2010. (Bahrain Center for Human Rights)

Blogger and activist **Abduljalil Alsingace** was detained in August 2010, allegedly because of national security concerns. After a visit to the United Kingdom, where he spoke to the House of Lords about human rights in Bahrain, he was arrested by security forces at the country's international airport. (CPJ)

In April, the Ministry of Information and Culture screened and in several cases blocked news updates sent over the **BlackBerry mobile network**. The ministry insisted that prior consent was needed before exchanging news via the network, prompting news media to claim the government was censoring any reports critical of the government. (International News Safety Institute)

Bangladesh

Authorities blocked Facebook on 29 May 2010 to prevent access to the **'Everybody Draw Mohammed Day'** group page, which asked visitors to post images of the prophet Mohammed on the website. Access to the site was resumed in June after images of the prophet were removed. Pakistani authorities also instructed local ISPs to block access earlier in the month. (CNET, RSF)

Belarus

The website of pro-democracy human rights organisation **Charter 97** came under distributed denial-of-service attacks in the run up to the 19 December election. One of the attacks followed the publication of an interview with opposition activist Andrei Sannikov in November and further attacks continued as the site attempted to publish news on protests and arrests following the election. The website's office was also vandalised during the post-election unrest. (Index on Censorship, *New York Times*)

Natalia Radzina, editor of opposition website Charter 97, was interrogated by officials regarding comments posted on the website on 6 July 2010. The comments expressed support for Afghan-Soviet veterans who refused medals from President Lukashenko. (RSF)

It was announced that citizens would require passports to use **internet cafes** from 1 July 2010. The decree also required all ISPs to store data on individual internet use for a year and to hand that information over to law enforcement agencies upon request. (RFE/RL)

Brazil

Prosecutors opened a formal investigation into paedophilia, defamation and reports of false identity involving social networking site **Orkut** on 21 July 2010. They demanded that Google, the site's owner, implement a system that stores internet protocol addresses, making it easier for authorities to track pages of those thought to be complicit in crime, giving them 120 days to carry out the work. In April 2010, it was announced that Google would have to pay damages for defamatory comments made about a priest, and in November 2009, it was sued for a fake profile of a famous sportsman. (*Independent*)

Burma

Web users and cybercafe owners reported that their connections were regularly cut or slowed down in the run up to the November elections. On 27 October, **Bagan Net** users reported that internet access was regularly interrupted or slowed down considerably. (Mizzima)

News websites operating in exile, including the **Democratic Voice of Burma**, **Mizzima** and *Irrawaddy* magazine, were hacked into on 27 September 2010. The attacks coincided with the three-year anniversary of the monk-led 'Saffron Revolution'. (Human Rights House)

Internet cafe owners in Pegu, near Rangoon, were ordered to keep records of personal profiles of users on 5 February 2010. The move was said to be for security reasons. (Mizzima)

Canada

A court ruled on 19 October 2010 that Google violated Canadian privacy law when it introduced **Street View** as part of its mapping services. The country's privacy commissioner said that citizens' rights had been violated when personal information was collected in preparation for launching the service. The commissioner ordered Google to delete confidential data and said it must comply with its security recommendations by 1 February 2011. (*Guardian*)

A blogger who accused Calgary police of 'perjury, corruption and destroying evidence' on his website was arrested on 16 September 2010. **John Kelly** faced charges of criminal libel, leading campaigners to criticise the country's libel laws. (*Calgary Beacon*, *Calgary Herald*)

China

Democracy activist **Bai Dongping** was arrested in Beijing on 27

November 2010 for inciting subversion after he posted a photo online of the 1989 pro-democracy demonstrations in Tiananmen Square. Despite his long history of campaigning in China, it was the first time the veteran campaigner and lawyer had been arrested, though he had been instructed by police to not attend high-profile events such as the 2008 Olympic Games. (Associated Press, *Guardian*)

Cheng Jianping was sentenced to a year in a labour camp for 'disrupting social order' on 18 November after she retweeted a satirical message that urged Chinese protesters to destroy the Japanese pavilion at the Shanghai Expo. Her fiancé claimed Cheng reposted a comment that originally appeared in his Twitter feed, retweeting it in mid-October. The comment was intended as a joke ridiculing anti-Japanese protesters whose numbers had grown ever since the two countries entered into a diplomatic row over disputed islands in the East China Sea. Cheng had also been detained by police in August after she supported democracy activist Liu Xianbin. (BBC, *Guardian*, Reuters)

Organisers were forced to cancel an annual blogging conference in Shanghai on 20-21 November following pressure from the authorities. **The Chinese Blogger Conference** attracts dozens of prominent online commentators, entrepreneurs and digital artists annually. The event is considered to be politically sensitive because some delegates voice criticism of the government's censorship policies. One of the organisers stated that the venue cancelled the event under pressure from an unknown arm of the government. (*Wall Street Journal*)

Those wishing to access websites banned in China were able to do so using **Amazon's Kindle**. In November 2010, Kindle was able to bypass the Great Firewall, despite

not being officially available in mainland China. Bloggers reported that they were able to access sites such as Twitter and Facebook. Experts noted that if the government did choose to block Kindle, it would not be difficult to do so. (AFP, BBC)

Police arrested **Mou Yanxi** on 27 October after she published a post on Twitter stating her intention to protest in support of democracy activist Liu Xiabao. Mou's arrest came amidst a wider crackdown on supporters of the jailed dissident following media speculation about who would collect Liu's Nobel Peace Prize at the ceremony in Oslo. Another Twitter user reported that Mou was later released but authorities had seized her mobile phone and computer. (*Guardian*, Thaindian News)

Following the 8 October 2010 announcement that the Nobel Peace Prize would be awarded to Liu Xiaobo, **internet searches** for the democracy activist and 'Nobel peace prize' were blocked by the Chinese government. Text messages containing Liu's name in Chinese were also barred. (AFP)

It was revealed on 28 September 2010 that the Apple Maps application on the **Chinese iPhone 4** only displays government-approved maps, unlike previous models. (Information Week)

Authorities announced on 3 September 2010 that owners of **microblogging websites** will be told to appoint 'self-discipline commissioners' in order to be responsible for censorship. Companies managing blogging sites were informed that they were responsible for monitoring and blocking material that could threaten China's security and social stability. (RSF)

A question and answer webpage on Hong Kong's Chinese-language **Google** website was blocked in some parts of mainland China on 3 August 2010. Visitors to the forum

had searched for information on topics considered to be sensitive, including the 1989 Tiananmen Square massacre and the future of the communist party. (Reuters)

Authorities arranged for surveillance technology systems to be installed in **internet cafes** in Tibet as of 1 August 2010. The local media reported that the scheme was already in place in Lhasa. (Eurasia Review)

On 22 June, the legislature reviewed a draft amendment to the law pertaining to **state secrets**. The head of the National Administration for the Protection of State Secrets said current laws were in need of updating in order to deal with the development of information technology. The new law will affect ISPs, users and internet cafes. (International Business Times, Xinhua)

On 14 May 2010, authorities in the Xinjiang region restored access to **internet sites** that had been blocked following ethnic riots in July 2009. (Associated Press)

Voice of Tibet radio transmissions were jammed by Chinese authorities on 22 April 2010. The Oslo-based station reported that transmissions were blocked after exiled Tibetans and others offered messages of condolence for those affected by the earthquake on 14 April. (Norwegian PEN)

In April 2010, **three people were jailed for posting material online** that supported a woman's call for an investigation into her daughter's death to be reopened. The girl was allegedly gang-raped and killed by people said to have connections with the city's police. Authorities had previously ruled her death was due to an abnormal pregnancy. The three individuals supporting the mother's efforts were jailed on defamation charges. (*Guardian*)

China Telecom rejected claims that it **re-directed a large amount of net**

traffic in April 2010. The allegation surfaced in a report presented to the US Congress, which said that for 18 minutes the traffic was redirected to Chinese servers. The report said the re-routing of data was caused due to incorrect routing information, but it was unclear whether the re-routing was intentional. (BBC, *Guardian*)

In an address to the national legislature in April 2010, the director of the State Council Information Office called for the reduction of **online anonymity**. Under the proposals, internet users will be forced to provide real names and details when posting comments on forums. (First Amendment Coalition, Human Rights in China, *New York Times*)

The **Foreign Correspondent Club of China** (FCCC) closed down their website on 2 April 2010 following denial-of-service attacks. There were also attacks on email addresses belonging to foreign correspondents working in the country over the same period. (BBC, CPJ)

On 31 March 2010, search terms containing the code string **'gs_rfai'** did not produce results when typed into the Google search engine. After an initial concern that the failure was a technical glitch, it was confirmed that the searches were being blocked by Chinese censors who may have assumed the letters 'rfa' were mistaken for Radio Free Asia, a search term not allowed in China. (*Telegraph*)

Refusing to comply with the Chinese government's censorship requirements, Google stopped its **internet search services** on mainland China on 23 March 2010, redirecting users to its unrestricted Hong Kong site. On 19 January, Google postponed the launch of a mobile phone incorporating its email and web services following disputes with the government over censorship and hacking of its internal network. (BBC, *Guardian*, *New York Times*)

The government ordered mobile phone companies in Beijing and Shanghai to suspend **text services** to phone users who send messages with 'illegal or unhealthy content' on 19 January. (*New York Times*)

On 21 February, an investigation into 2009 cyber attacks against **Google** and other American companies traced the interruption of service to computers at two Chinese academic institutions. The distinguished Jiaotong University and Lanxiang Vocational School in Shandong Province, which has ties to the military, both denied involvement in the attacks, which affected email addresses of human rights activists and corporate employees. (*Guardian*, *New York Times*)

On 6 and 7 February 2010, police in central China arrested three people and seized money and equipment in a crackdown on the country's biggest commercial operation to train **computer hackers**. Experts in cyber attacks doubted that the move represented any real effort on the government's part to tackle breaches in online security, as authorities did not shut down servers thought to be used in large scale attacks or those who operate them. (*Guardian*, *New York Times*)

Human rights advocates including **Ai Weiwei** and **Teng Biao** reported that their Gmail accounts had been infiltrated on 19 January 2010. (*Guardian*)

The government blocked access to online film database **imdb.com** on 7 January 2010. In the same week, there were reports that other sites were running slowly, leading to the belief that the censorship board was updating its technologies. (*Examiner*)

Colombia

Ex-President Alvaro Uribe launched a libel suit against a **former senator** who posted comments about him on Twitter. The senator allegedly accused Uribe of being linked to the murder of a presidential aide. (*El Tiempo*)

Egypt

Service provider Noor was shut down on 1 February 2011 after the other major service providers, Link Egypt, Vodaphone/Raya, Telecom Egypt and Etisalat Misr suspended services on 27 January. Text messages sent via mobile phones were also disabled. The virtual **communications blackout** followed days of protests calling for the resignation or removal of President Mubarak. Internet and text messaging services resumed on 3 February. (Channel 4 News)

Access to **Twitter** was banned on 25 January 2011 as Tunisian-inspired protests erupted in Cairo and other Egyptian cities. Vodafone Egypt and TEData also blocked mobile internet. (BBC)

Prominent blogger **Kareem Amer** was released from prison on 15 Novemeber 2010 after serving a four-year sentence for insulting Islam and defaming President Hosni Mubarak, who he referred to as a 'dictator'. Charged with inciting hatred of Islam, he was the first Egyptian convicted for material published online. After his arrest in 2006, he was also expelled from university in Alexandria. He was released two weeks after his official sentence ended and there were reports that he had been physically attacked during his incarceration. (BBC, Reuters)

In mid-October, the national telecommunications regulator set new rules for private production companies sending **text messages** to multiple mobile phones. The new laws were seen as a direct effort to reduce reform groups and other political campaigners from mobilising support in the run up to the November elections. (al Jazeera)

In mid-September, **Amr Osama**'s blog was closed by the free Emirati hosting service provider. The ban followed the publication of a post that cited politician Omar Soliman as a potential presidential candidate. (ANHRI)

Blogger and activist **Musaad Suliman Hassan Hussein** was released from prison on 13 July 2010 after being held without trial under emergency laws for three years. He had been accused of 'inciting others to protest', and 'assaulting public officers during the exercise of their duties'. (Amnesty International)

Blogger and publisher **Ahmed Mahanna** was arrested and his house raided on 3 April 2010 following the publication of a book entitled *ElBaradei And The Dream of The Green Revolution* by Kamal Gobrial. He was released the next day. (ANHRI, *Guardian*)

Newsroom employees for **IslamOnline** staged a mass walkout on 17 March 2010 after its new directors proposed a more religious and conservative editorial line. The website is run by a non-governmental organisation based in Qatar. (*Guardian*, Timesonline)

Ethiopia

Voice of America's Amharic-language internet radio broadcasts were blocked on 22 February 2010. The jamming of the site's news services affected all five of the network's shortwave frequencies in the country. (nazret.com)

European Union

In March 2010, the European Commission proposed that **websites** containing child pornography should be blocked across the EU. The measure formed part of a legislative package to combat human trafficking and the sexual exploitation of children. But some politicians, including Germany's justice minister, said removal of sites

was more effective method of reducing access to sites, adding that blocking sites led to mistrust between internet users and governments. (EU Observer, European Voice)

France

WikiLeaks' main server in France went offline on 5 December 2010 after France's industry minister stated that the country should not host a site that violated diplomatic relations. (AP)

A court found **Google** guilty of libel in late September. A convicted sex offender who was granted anonymity sued the company after his name was linked to offensive words including 'rapist' and 'Satanist'. The company was fined €5,000 (US$6,700). (Radio France International)

French lawmakers took steps in mid-February 2010 to increase **online filtering**. The draft law allows for police to wiretap internet networks and phone lines and would force ISPs to filter internet traffic. (the Inquirer, PC World)

Gambia

The publishers of the US-based **Gambia Echo** reported that the Gambian government had blocked access to its website within the Gambia. The newspaper informed the US State Department that President Yahya Jammeh's government was denying access to the site. (Media Foundation for West Africa)

Germany

Thousands of people demonstrated in Berlin on 11 September 2010, protesting against **surveillance, data retention and lack of transparency** in government. The protest was one of several across Europe. (AFP)

After the country's data protection authority (DPA) requested that

Google audit the data collected by its **Street View** cars, the company issued a statement online on 14 May admitting that it had inadvertently collected sensitive private data sent over WiFi networks. (Huffington Post)

Ghana

On 31 May 2010, the opposition group Alliance for Accountable Governance (AFAG) sued the Ghanaian National Communications Authority (NCA), the country's attorney general and all mobile telephone operators over the proposed installation of a **monitoring device**. AFAG claimed the plans violated privacy laws. The writ specifically demanded the Human Rights Court in Accra declare the device 'illegal' and 'unconstitutional'. (Ghana News Now)

India

In February 2011, the government ordered telecom operators to suspend all mobile messaging services that cannot be monitored by law enforcement agencies, citing national security reasons. The government had given **Research In Motion** (RIM), the BlackBerry's Canadian manufacturer, until 31 January to provide it with access to encrypted data on BlackBerry Enterprise Server. RIM says it is unable to do so as it does not hold the keys to the encrypted data. In 2010, RIM had provided the government with the ability to monitor some of its other services, including BlackBerry Messenger and email. (*Times of India*)

Indonesia

Human rights websites fell victim to cyber attacks on 28 October 2010 after posting a video of soldiers torturing two Papuan tribesmen. **Survival International** and the **Asian Human Rights Commission** were among the organisations under attack. (Digital Journal, *Guardian*)

More than 200 internet service providers agreed to block **pornographic websites** and sites featuring nudity during the holy month of Ramadan in August 2010. The Technology and Communications Minister said it would be impossible to be place a complete ban on sites publishing pornography (*Jakarta Post*)

Musician **Nazril 'Ariel' Irham** could face up to 12 years under anti-pornography laws after he allegedly appeared in amateur sex videos with two women on the internet. Ariel went into police custody in June 2010 and all three deny appearing in the videos. (BBC)

International

On 9 December 2010, activist group Anonymous launched an online assault on the websites of credit companies *MasterCard* and *Visa* after group financial services to **WikiLeaks** were discontinued. Similar attacks were launched on the websites of Sarah Palin and Joe Lieberman, two of the most vocal critics of WikiLeaks in the United States (BBC, Guardian).

On 15 November 2010, Google's director of public policy urged western governments to **challenge internet censorship** in countries such as China. A policy brief on internet trade stated that 'more than 40 governments' restricted information on a large scale, and came at the end of a year in which Google struggled with the Chinese government over demands for it to comply with the country's strict censorship laws. In March 2010, it announced that it would no longer censor search results on google.cn. (googlepublicpolicy.blogspot, *Guardian*)

In August 2010, some human rights groups, including Amnesty International, called on **WikiLeaks** to redact their Afghan war files so that the names of individual Afghans would not appear. (BBC)

In June 2010, internet overseer ICANN voted in favour of creating **.xxx**, a pornography-specific web domain. Some critics of the move warned that it will make sex more accessible online, whilst others argued that it will make government censorship of online material easier. (Bizcommunity)

Foreign ministers from France and the Netherlands set up a working group to devise an **international code of conduct** to address internet censorship in late May 2010. The project aimed to protect freedom on the internet and brings together governments, human rights activists and online businesses. (Radio Netherlands, *Sydney Morning Herald*)

On 23 April, Google published a webpage displaying which governments request **private user data** or demand that content is removed. (Geek, *Guardian*)

Iran

Google lifted some of its **restrictions for online users** in the country on 21 January 2011. Users were able to access previously restricted services including Google Chrome, Google Earth and Picasa following sanctions by the American government. The restrictions were still in place for users linked to the Iranian government. (Radio Farda)

The trial of 18-year-old blogger **Navid Mohebbi** began on 14 November 2010 in Amol. Mohebbi was arrested by intelligence ministry personnel in September after being harassed on several occasions throughout the year. His charges include acting against national security and insulting leaders of the Islamic republic. An activist for women's rights in Iran, Mohebbi was also charged with involvement in the 'One Million Signatures Campaign', which works to promote gender equality. He was given a suspended three-year sentence and released on 25 December. (Bikya Masr, RSF)

Doctor and blogger **Mehdi Khazali**, the son of a prominent conservative cleric, was arrested in Tehran on 14 October 2010. He was charged with 'acting against national security and disturbing public opinion'. His website is openly critical of President Mahmoud Ahmadinejad. During the 2009 post-election protests he spent 23 days in solitary confinement. (AFP)

The public testing of **Haystack**, software designed to provide Iranians with uncensored access to the internet, was suspended in September 2010 after experts voiced security concerns. The Haystack project was devised in 2009 following the government crackdown and increased online filtering in response to mass protests. (Softpedia)

The government revealed plans to establish an **internet police force** in mid-June. The head of the security forces, Major General Esmaeel Ahmadi Moghadam said its purpose would be to 'identify threats and remove them'. (CNN)

In February 2010, authorities announced a permanent block on access to **Google Mail**, adding that there were plans to create a national email service. The move was seen as part of a wider crackdown in the run up to the anniversary of the Iranian revolution. Internet traffic was also said to be running extremely slowly, raising suspicions amongst free expression advocates. The government claimed a technical fault was responsible for the slow service (CPJ, RSF)

Human rights activists **Mehrdad Rahimi** and **Kouhyar Goudarzi** were accused of waging 'a war against God' and told they could face the death penalty in late January 2010. Both contributed to an opposition website and faced possible death penalties. (RSF)

Ireland

On 2 June 2010, one of the country's main internet providers, Eircom, became the first telecoms company in Europe to introduce a 'graduated response' procedure under which **clients who download music illegally** could end up losing their connection. (European Digital Rights, RSF)

Following a freedom of information request, it was revealed on 16 April 2010 that the government was discussing introducing **internet blocking**. The plans are thought to be underway in order to block illegal websites including child pornography, but industry experts have complained that the effectiveness of such initiatives are limited, while the likelihood of disrupting services to general users is high. (*Irish Times*)

Israel

Internet service provider 012 Smile started censoring the internet by **restricting access to online gambling sites** on 18 August 2010. The filter was put in place as a response to an injunction lodged by police in July. (*Haaretz*)

Italy

An investigation into **illegal wiretapping** by the brother of Prime Minister Silvio Berlusconi began in early June 2010. Paolo Berlusconi was under investigation for publishing information about politicians obtained via unwarranted wiretaps in his newspaper *Il Giornale*. (*Independent*)

Lawmakers called for amendments to a controversial draft **internet law** on 3 February 2010. The law, if passed, would have meant that the internet would be regarded as a conventional television broadcaster, responsible for all editorial content and required to obtain a licence. (European Digital Rights, Infoworld)

Ivory Coast

Saint Claver Oula, **Stéphane Guédé** and **Théophile Kouamouo**

were arrested on 13 July 2010 following the online publication of leaked reports concerning corruption in the country's cocoa and coffee trade. Authorities were reported to have pressured the journalists to reveal the source of the leak. (Global Voices)

Japan

On 24 December 2010, the Ministry of Internal Affairs and Communications requested that Apple and SoftBank Mobile Corp, the service provider for Apple's iPhone, devise and install content filtering software on **iPhone** with immediate effect. The ministry stated that the new software would prevent users from gaining access to dangerous content, insisting that the iPhone did not provide adequate control options to prevent minors from accessing content intended for adults. The industry criticised the decision, pointing out that the process for individual users' registration for downloading the software would be cumbersome and impractical. (Yomiuri Shimbun)

Jordan

On 5 August 2010, the government blocked more than 40 independent **websites** in public sector workplaces. Many of the websites reported on issues not covered in other aspects of the media, including workers' rights and conditions for teachers. (ANHRI)

The Interior Ministry issued new instructions to tighten control on **internet cafes** on 7 June 2010. Cafe owners were instructed to prevent access to sites featuring pornography and criticism of religion, and to sites that promote drugs, tobacco or gambling. (ANHRI)

Kazakhstan

After the government introduced laws allowing courts to block **websites** in 2009, it was reported in April 2010 that Opera, a web browser that bypasses censors, became the most popular way to access the

internet in the country. Internet users were unable to access a range of websites featuring content critical of the government without using a browser using circumvention software. (*Independent*, Reuters)

Kosovo

The telecommunications authority began removing communications network equipment belonging to Serbian mobile operators in the region on 26 September 2010. Many of the antennas were thought to be operating illegally, but the removal of them left thousands of minority Serbs without **landline or mobile service**. (SETimes.com, Telegeography)

Kuwait

On 3 August 2010, the government asked BlackBerry's Research in Motion Ltd (RIM) to block **pornographic websites**. They stopped short of threatening to suspend messenger services as other countries in the Gulf did. RIM approved the blocking of 3,000 sites. (Reuters)

Libya

Twitter, **Facebook**, and **al Jazeera** were among websites blocked on 18 February 2011. Reacting to protests in Benghazi and elsewhere, the government ordered an official news blackout and there were widespread reports that the internet had been completely shut down. On 16 February, writer and blogger **Mohamed Ashim** was detained; his mobile phone and computer were both confiscated. The director and editor-in-chief of **Irassa**, a local news website, were questioned by security forces. (al Arabiya, CPJ, *Guardian*, Techcrunch)

Morocco

Blogger and activist **Kacem el Ghazzali** received death threats on 10 September 2010. His writing, published on website Bahmout, discusses controversial topics including secularism. In April, the Facebook site run by the blogger was inaccessible. (Global Voices)

Nepal

Online journalist **Shreedeep Rayamajhi** was physically attacked on 24 December 2010. Rayamajhi, who writes for GroundReport and other news websites, began receiving threats for his work in June and had been attacked previously. (Global Voices)

North Korea

Foreign visitors were banned from renting **mobile phones** in January 2011. The move was thought by many to be an attempt to restrict information getting into the country concerning unrest in the Middle East and some parts of Africa. Authorities do not allow visitors to bring mobile phones into the country upon their arrival. (Radio Netherlands)

Pakistan

The government blocked **YouTube** on 20 May 2010 due to 'sacrilegious' content. Access to **Flickr** and **Wikipedia** was also restricted. (*Guardian*)

On 19 May 2010, the Pakistani Telecommunication Authority locked access to **Facebook** by order of the government. The ban was in response to the 'Everybody Draw Mohammed Day' page on the site, which encouraged members to uploaded images of the prophet Mohammed. (CNN)

Russia

On 2 August 2010, the Russian government followed the UAE and considered banning **BlackBerries** because the encryption software used on its email, instant messaging and web browsing services. Talks began between the authorities and RIM. (*Guardian, Independent*)

A court in Komsomolsk-on-Amur ordered an internet provider to block five sites on 29 July 2010 after concerns were raised over videos featuring ultra-nationalist material. The blocked sites included **YouTube**, owned by Google. The company responded, saying the move restricted access to information. (*Guardian*, Reuters)

Saudi Arabia

The Ministry of Information and Culture announced on 22 September 2010 that **web publishers**, including online media, blogs and forums, must register with the government and obtain a licence. Spokesman Abdul Rahman al Hazza said the measure would reduce libel and defamation. (TechCrunch)

New **regulations on electronic publishing** came into effect on 1 January 2010. The new law required anyone posting material online to obtain a press licence and abide by content limitation regulations that ban 'offending others', 'compromising the economy or security' and disobedience to Islamic Law. (ANHRI)

Singapore

The government stated on 29 September that it would not lift a ban on **100 websites**, ignoring recommendations from its Censorship Review Committee (CRC). The CRC had suggested replacing the ban with an optional filtering service. (Business Week)

South Africa

Regulations to restrict access to **pornography online** and via mobile phones were referred to the Law Reform Commission on 27 May 2010 by deputy minister of home affairs Malusi Gigaba. (allAfrica)

South Korea

Police restricted access to **64 websites** that had been classified as 'pro-North Korean' on 13 December 2010. The websites, many of which contain photographs of the North Korean leader and articles from the North's official newspaper *Rodong Sinmun* were accused of supporting North Korean 'military-first' ideology and inciting rebellion. South Korea's law National Security Act prohibits 'anti-state acts'. Site owners changed the web addresses of many of the websites in an attempt to resume access. (Chosun Ilbo)

In August 2010, South Korea blocked access to a **Twitter** account registered to a North Korean website. The blocking appeared to be aimed solely at the account of @Uriminzok, which has provided North Korea with a platform for propaganda messages and is thought to be run by the North Korean government. (Softpedia)

Spain

The Spanish Agency for Data Protection (AEPD) announced on 18 October 2010 that it had sued Google over its **Street View** service for alleged violation of the country's data protection laws. Filing the suit, the AEPD said it had evidence of five offences committed by Google involving the capturing and storing of data from users connected to Wi-Fi networks. (the *Age*)

Syria

In February 2011, blogger **Tal al Mallouhi** was sentenced to five years in prison by a state security court on espionage charges. The blogger, who was accused of spying on behalf of the United States, had already been detained for 14 months at the time of the hearing. Her blogs mainly concerned the political and humanitarian situation in Palestine. The charges against her are thought to be based on a letter she sent to President Obama concerning his stance on the Arab world and Islam and an invitation to attend an event at the US embassy in Cairo. (Bikya Masr, CNN)

Thailand

In May 2010, the government closed down news website's **Prachtai**'s Facebook page. The site's editor, **Chiranuch Premchaipoen**, was arrested in September for insulting the monarchy. She was released on bail with the proviso that she reported to police every month until her trial. In February 2011, the trial was postponed to accommodate the long list of witnesses expected to give evidence. (RSF, *New York Times*)

On 18 August 2010, authorities restricted access to the **WikiLeaks** website on security grounds. The restrictions were introduced under the 2005 emergency decree as an attempt to avoid political unrest following riots earlier in the year. (AP)

King Bhumibol Adulyadej pardoned **Suvicha Thakhor** on 28 June 2010. Thakhor was arrested in April 2009 and had been serving a 10-year prison sentence on a lèse majesté charge for allegedly modifying photographs of the royal family and posting them online. (RSF)

Trinidad and Tobago

On 12 November, the prime minister announced she had learned the Security Intelligence Agency (SIA) had been **illegally tapping telephones and intercepting emails** without the public's knowledge. The SIA, which was set up by the previous government, targeted, among others, politicians, judges, trade unionists, entertainment personalities and journalists. Following the prime minister's statement to parliament, in which she stated that she had not been aware of what she termed the 'covert project', the government took steps to legalise operations of the SIA. In mid-December, the controversial Interception of Communications Act, which makes it legal to wiretap on grounds of national security, was introduced. (Government of Trinidad & Tobago website, RSF, the *Trinidad Guardian*)

Tunisia

The Tunisian Internet Agency attempted to hack into **Sofiene Chourabi**'s Facebook account on 6 January 2011. Chourabi, a journalist for *al Tariq al Jadid* magazine and a blogger known for his criticism of authorities, claimed that the government body had blocked access to his page on the social networking site since 2009 and that his blogs are inaccessible within the country. (al Jazeera, CPJ)

In December 2010 and January 2011, anti-government demonstrators used social media including blogs, Twitter and Facebook to disseminate news about protest developments and police brutality. The sites were also used to schedule protests. On 1 January 2011, the government reacted by hacking into users' **gmail** and **Facebook** accounts and blocking popular **websites** including **Flickr, Wat.tv, Blip.tv, Agoravox.fr** and a number of blogs. International 'hacktivist' group Anonymous targeted government websites, including that of the president, prime minister and stock exchange on 2 January 2011. (al Jazeera, Index on Censorship)

Turkey

Following a complaint from the presidential office, founder of Haberin Yeri website **Cem Büyükçakır** was given an 11-month jail sentence on 4 November 2010 for publishing a reader's comment implying that President Abdullah Gül descended from an Armenian family. The charges were applied despite the fact that Büyükçakır removed the offending comment as soon as he received a warning that it might be in violation of the criminal code. The reader's comment was originally posted on the site the end of 2008. (Bianet)

The government lifted a two-year ban on the **YouTube** website at the end of October 2010 after a court found that the videos that had originally warranted the ban had been removed. But on 1 November, Google reposted the videos, which were considered to be offensive about the republic's founder Mustafa Kemal Atatürk. YouTube is one of thousands of websites banned in Turkey. The country's internet law enables entire sites to be banned if any amount of material on them is found to infringe on a range of banned topics, from obscenity to insulting Atatürk. (BBC, *Wall Street Journal*)

Research In Motion Ltd (RIM) faced a ban of its **BlackBerry data services** on 24 October 2010 for non-compliance with legislation requiring all manufacturers to hand over communication encryption keys to authorities. The law allows the Information and Communication Technologies Authority to collect the algorithms and keys from every hardware provider offering encrypted telecommunications capabilities. (Softpedia)

Dozens of international organisations appealed to the Turkish government to lift bans on **Google and internet services** in June 2010, and thereby align with international standards pertaining to internet laws. Anti-censorship hackers protested by disrupting access to government internet addresses including that of the Ministry of Transportation and Information and Communication Technologies Authority. (Bianet, CyberLaw blog, the New New Internet)

A **student** received an 11-month suspended jail sentence on 10 May 2010 for posting a cartoon of the mayor of the city of Eskisehir on Facebook. He was charged under one of the country's defamation laws. (RSF)

United Arab Emirates

A ban on **BlackBerry services** scheduled for 11 October was suspended after the Telecommunications

Regulatory Authority declared that the company complied with the necessary regulations. (BBC)

In July 2010, authorities harassed and arrested **BlackBerry users** after a group of people allegedly tried to use the mobile service to organise a protest march against an increase in the price of petrol. (RSF)

United Kingdom

The first fines for **breaches of the Data Protection Act** were issued in late November 2010. Hertfordshire County Council was fined after it accidentally faxed details of a child sex abuse case to a member of the public and a company; a Sheffield-based company was fined for losing a laptop containing personal details of thousands of people. (BBC)

Members of Parliament scheduled a debate on **pornography online** in late November 2010 after Conservative MP Claire Perry called for regulations to be introduced. The 'opt-in' system would require internet providers to use age verification to allow access to pornography in order to prevent children from accessing inappropriate images. (BBC)

The anti-police surveillance website **fitwatch.org.uk** was suspended at the request of the Metropolitan Police's public order section on 15 November 2010. The police stated that the site was being used as a forum for planning illegal activities. The blog posted guidance to students who worried they might be arrested following the occupation of the Millbank office complex, which houses Conservative Party headquarters. The website was set up in 2007 by protesters opposing surveillance tactics used by Forward Intelligence Teams. (*Guardian*, Index on Censorship)

The information commissioner issued a statement on 3 November 2010 announcing that Google committed

a 'significant breach' of the Data Protection Act by intercepting Wi-fi information when setting up its **Street View** service. He rejected calls to inflict a financial penalty on Google, but insisted the company must ensure data protection breaches did not re-occur. The commissioner reconsidered an earlier ruling that Google was not in breach after the Canadian data agency found the search engine to be in breach of its laws. (BBC, Computer Weekly, *Guardian*)

In August 2010, a family won their case against a local council who kept them under surveillance from 10 February to 3 March 2008. Monitoring started after the council received an anonymous tip-off that the family were not living in the catchment area of an oversubscribed local school. (BBC)

On 13 August, Moneybookers, a British-registered internet payment company, informed **WikiLeaks** that it was closing its account because the organisation appeared on a US financial securities watchlist. A few days earlier, the Pentagon expressed its anger at Wikileaks and its founder for leaking thousands of classified documents about the war in Afghanistan. (*Guardian*)

On 9 April 2010, **Stuart MacLennan**, a Labour parliamentary candidate, was forced to step down after he posted inappropriate comments on Twitter. MacLennan apologised and closed his account on the site after making offensive comments about the elderly, politicians and celebrities. (*Telegraph*)

United States

The Obama administration blocked hundreds of thousands of federal workers from accessing the **WikiLeaks** website on 3 December 2010. The leaked cables were available elsewhere online, but employees were prevented from accessing the WikiLeaks site directly, as the

material was still considered to be classified material. (BBC, Guardian)

Amazon, which hosted the website **WikiLeaks**, took the website off its server on 2 December 2010 following political pressure from the US government and others. Shortly thereafter, California-based provider Everydns also pulled down the site. It reappeared later the same day, using a Swiss domain and a list of mirror sites was also published online in an effort to provide constant access to the site. (BBC, *Guardian*)

On October 24 2010, a software developer released an add-on for Firefox that allowed users to access the accounts of others on their local network. Firesheep, created by Eric Butler, was intended to highlight a flaw in **internet security** and force susceptible websites to make themselves more secure. Butler regarded Microsoft's move to detect Firesheep as part of its anti-virus application as censorship. (*Wired*)

At the end of September 2010, national security officials and federal law enforcement employees expressed their support for proposed legislation that would require phone and broadband companies to make lines more accessible to **wiretapping**. Officials argued that amendments were essential because of technological developments and system upgrades that caused technical problems for surveillance. A task force was set up to draft an expansion of the Communications Assistance to Law Enforcement Act, a 1994 law that demands that telephone and broadband companies must design their services so that surveillance of a target can begin immediately following the presentation of a court order. (*New York Times*)

There were reports on 6 August 2010 that content uploaded to link-sharing website **Digg** was 'censored' by a group referred to as 'Digg Patriots'. The group was said to have systematically downgraded 'liberal' stories. (*Guardian*)

The Obama administration took steps to make it easier for the FBI to compel companies to turn over records of an individual's **internet activity** without a court order on 29 July 2010. Government lawyers stated that 'electronic communication transactional records' would be added to the list of materials agents can obtain if they believe the information is relevant to a terrorism or intelligence investigation. (*Washington Post*)

A website hosting 70,000 bloggers was closed without warning on 20 July 2010 after terrorist material, including bomb-making instructions, was found on one of its sites. Burstnet closed down the **Blogetry** site without warning. (BBC)

Apple banned an **iPhone application** based on the website ChatRoulette on 19 July 2010. The move followed complaints that users exposed themselves to strangers in an inappropriate manner while using the program. (Cult of Mac)

On 30 June, a court in New Jersey ruled that laws protecting journalists did not apply to bloggers. **Shellee Hale** attempted to use the state's shield law to protect herself in a defamation case but was told that she would not be protected because she was not affiliated with a 'legitimate' news organisation. The case was lodged following comments Hale posted on an internet message board about an adult entertainment company. (Citizen Law Project, Digital Journal)

Private Bradley Manning, who was arrested in May 2010 for leaking video footage of an Apache helicopter strike in Baghdad to WikiLeaks, was formally charged on 6 July. (RFERL)

The Washington Supreme Court ruled in May 2010 that libraries that chose to filter **internet access** were not in violation of citizens' right to free expression. Following complaints lodged by three library users who found they could not access sites at their local libraries, the court ruled that libraries do not have to provide access to all material is protected under the constitution. (Ars Technica)

Venezuela

The creation of a new government agency was announced ahead of the September 2010 legislative elections. A presidential decree announced the move, which gives the agency power to suppress or curtail 'any information' deemed to be of national interest. Free expression advocates viewed the move as a sign of renewed pressure on news critical of the government. (Knight Center)

Miami-based internet radio stations **CaracasRadioTV** and **Radionexx** were blocked in September 2010. On 26 September, there were reports that blogging website WordPress was also blocked for a period of three days. (Informaction Civica)

Luis Enrique Acosta and **Carmen Cecilia Nares** were arrested on 8 July 2010 after they posted critiques on the health of the country's banking sector on Twitter. They were arrested under a 2001 banking law against 'disseminating false rumours'. (Reuters, RSF)

Vietnam

Popular blogger **LeNguyen Huong Tra**, who blogs under the name Do Long Girl, was arrested on 23 October 2010 in Ho Chi Minh City for allegedly insulting a senior communist party official and his family. Her blog often tackles politically sensitive issues, and on 14 October she posted a story about an official granting favours to women who had romantic relations with his son. (CPJ)

Political blogger **Phan Thanh Hai** was arrested on 18 October, charged with publishing false information. Police also raided the blogger's home, seizing computers and documents. The arrest was seen as the as part of a wider crackdown on dissident journalists critical of the government. (AFP, CPJ)

On 30 September, blogger **Pham Minh Hoang** was charged with attempting to overthrow the government and membership to a terrorist organisation. The arrest was thought to be related to his opposition to bauxite mining by a Chinese company in the Lang Son region. (RSF)

Internet users in Vietnam complained that their access to the **BBC** website and **Facebook** had been blocked in June 2010. (Asia News, Intellasia)

Zambia

In June 2010, police officers allegedly searched the mobile phone records of **journalists** in an attempt to discover their sources. The instructions to conduct the searches were said to have come from Inspector General Francis Kabonde, Zambia's most senior policeman. (*Zambia Post*)

Compiled by William Clowes, Martin Dudas, Ramin Namvari and Mi Kyoung Park
Edited by Natasha Schmidt
DOI: 10.1177/0306422011400798

Connect, Debate, Engage

nnouncing three new online communities....

Connect with other researchers and
discuss your research interests

Keep up with announcements in the field,
for example call for papers and jobs

Discover and review resources

- Engage with featured content
  such as key articles, podcasts
  and videos

- Find out about relevant conferences
  and events

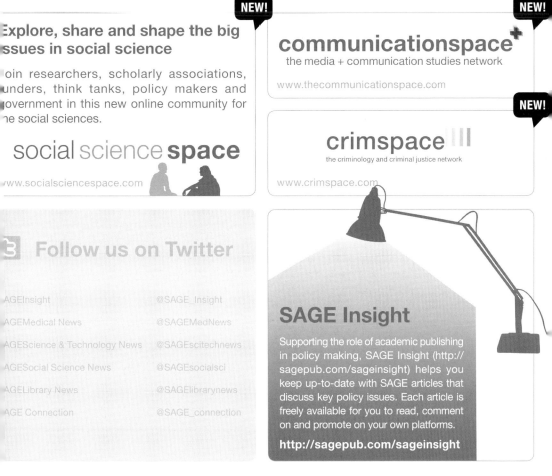

NEW!

**Explore, share and shape the big
ssues in social science**

oin researchers, scholarly associations,
unders, think tanks, policy makers and
jovernment in this new online community for
he social sciences.

social science **space**

ww.socialsciencespace.com

communicationspace⁺
the media + communication studies network

www.thecommunicationspace.com

NEW!

crimspace
the criminology and criminal justice network

www.crimspace.com

3 Follow us on Twitter

AGEInsight   @SAGE_Insight

AGEMedical News   @SAGEMedNews

AGEScience & Technology News   @SAGEscitechnews

AGESocial Science News   @SAGEsocialsci

AGELibrary News   @SAGELibrarynews

AGE Connection   @SAGE_connection

SAGE Insight

Supporting the role of academic publishing
in policy making, SAGE Insight (http://
sagepub.com/sageinsight) helps you
keep up-to-date with SAGE articles that
discuss key policy issues. Each article is
freely available for you to read, comment
on and promote on your own platforms.

http://sagepub.com/sageinsight

sit our website for a complete list of all our social media activities:
ttp://www.sagepub.com/socialmedia

THAI TRIALS

The internet has become an important forum for dissent in Thailand and the latest casualty in an increasingly divided society, says **Supinya Klangnarong**

Since the military coup in 2006, Thai netizens have become a significant voice of dissent. Online forums will openly tackle subjects censored in the traditional print and electronic media, especially the taboo against discussing the monarchy. In response, the government has taken steps to limit freedom online in the name of national security. The Computer Crime Act (CCA) was passed in 2007 and researchers at the iLaw project have shown that there have been 117 court orders to block access to more than 74,000 URLs. The largest number of blocked websites contains content considered offensive to the monarchy (57,330), followed at some distance by pornography (16,740). In addition, there were 184 prosecutions, including fraud, defamation and lèse majesté (insulting the monarchy). The government has also set up 'cyber scout' units to monitor the internet for inappropriate content. When a state of emergency was declared during the protests last year, the government was able to block sites without a court order.

One of the most notorious, current cases is the prosecution of Chiranuch Premchaiporn, the director of independent news website prachatai.com. She

A portrait of King Bhumibol Adulyadej on the side of a shopping mall in Bangkok, November 2007
Credit: Roy Garner/Alamy

was arrested in 2009 and charged under the CCA for comments posted on one of Prachatai's discussion forums, which were allegedly critical of a member of the royal family. She was arrested for a second time last September (on her way back from an internet freedom conference in Europe) and now also faces prosecution under the lèse majesté law. Once again, the cause of the complaint sprang from comments posted on Prachatai's discussion board. She could face up to 20 years in jail. Depending on the outcome, it's likely to be a test case for intermediary liability in Thailand.

Although access to computers in Thailand lags far behind television – only 7 per cent of the population has access to computers, compared with 95.5 per cent to television – the number of online users has increased by 15.5 per cent over the past year. The popularity of social networks has also tripled in the same time: Twitter and Facebook played an important role for citizen journalism during the unrest in April and May last year, covering events in areas unreported in the mainstream media.

The government's measures have emboldened the growing netizen movement to campaign for free speech online, but there is a marked chilling effect as well. It is an offence even to forward material that is considered a threat to national security or public order. As a result, online users have become more cautious.

Thai society is deeply divided, split between the demands of the royalist, anti-Thaksin Shinawatra yellow camp and the pro-Thaksin red camp, which opposed the 2006 coup. The divide cuts across the elite military, bureaucratic and business networks and academics, students, the media and grassroots' movements. Between these two groups lies a large silent majority that feels confused and frustrated by the continuing conflict, hoping for a way out.

The media – old and new – has become the battleground for both camps in an intense social conflict that has politicised debate about the role of the monarchy as never before. Thongthong Chandrangsu, a well-known royalist and historian of the monarchy, has even criticised the broad use of the infamous lèse-majesté law: 'I don't see the letter of the law as problematic, but the application of it is, when used in an all-encompassing way.' The historian Nidhi Eiewsriwong has pointed out that Thailand has still to reach a consensus on the dividing line between the protection of the monarchy and the protection of citizens' rights to freedom of expression. Nidhi maintains that the 'sacred space' in which the monarchy is revered must be reduced to fit a democratic system. 'If the sacred space is too large it will occupy and reduce the public's space.'

The country is reaching a turning point. The sub-culture of netizens presents an opportunity for developing an open society. But in a semi-democratic system, where the protection of national security and public morality shapes the social norms, it is very difficult to see a possible compromise. How many netizens will be forced to become dissidents if the Thai authorities continue to suppress freedom of expression? ☐

©Supinya Klangnarong
40(1): 122/124
DOI: 10.177/0306422011399823

Supinya Klangnarong is a media-policy advocate and visiting lecturer based in Bangkok. She is vice-chair of the Campaign for Popular Media Reform (CPMR) and a board member of Thai Netizen Network, an independent network of internet citizens working to uphold cyber liberty in Thailand

PYONGYANG UNWRAPPED

Technology has revolutionised reporting on North Korea. **David McNeill** reveals how a clandestine network is getting the word out despite restrictions

North Korea remains one of the world's black holes: a vast sealed experiment in information control. According to Reporters Without Borders, just 4 per cent of the population has access to the country's heavily censored internet, which is entirely under state control, along with all newspapers, radio and television. Visitors must surrender cell phones and mobile transmitters at the border.

On a visit last September with a group of undercover journalists, we could only send short emails from the five-star Yanggakdo hotel by giving the recipient's address to a clerk, who typed it into a computer (and charged a euro per line of message). 'What the North Koreans have access to is an "intranet" – it looks and feels like the internet, there are websites, but it's totally cut off from the rest of the world,' explains Martyn Williams, a reporter for IDG News Service who runs the northkoreatech.org blog. 'It's not connected to anything beyond the borders.'

Naturally, that makes verifying the scant information that trickles out a vexing matter. 'You could write a book – or at least a doctoral dissertation – on the lies that have been written about North Korea,' says Richard

Lloyd Parry, Asia correspondent for *The Times*. For years, says Lloyd Parry, it was assumed that Kim Jong-il was mentally ill, an alcoholic, a sex maniac or a psychopath. 'Then during the Inter-Korea forum in 2000, there he was on television, obviously fond of a drink but making sense and in control of the situation.'

Over the years, reporters have used strategy, ingenuity and plain subterfuge to peer through the black propaganda and get a clearer picture of life inside the country. Some enter North Korea with government officials or as tourists. Others draw on interviews with defectors for information, including *LA Times* correspondent Barbara Demick in her acclaimed book *Nothing to Envy*. Until recently, employing North Koreans as reporters was considered far-fetched, even revolutionary. But technological developments in the last few years have made that a possibility. Mobile phones, mini-cameras and recording devices are increasingly being smuggled out, and the dissenting voices of North Koreans themselves broadcast back into the country.

The implications are potentially profound, says longtime Pyongyang watcher Bradley K. Martin, author of *Under the Loving Care of the Fatherly Leader: North Korea and the Kim Dynasty*. 'A stepped-up campaign of providing accurate news about their own country and the rest of the world to a people who are no longer hermetically sealed off from such news could, over time, threaten the regime's domestic control.'

That's certainly the goal of Kim Seong-Min, who once wrote poems eulogising the North's military until he was accused of spying against the regime and defected. He now runs Free North Korea Radio (FNKR) in Seoul and wants to bring democracy to his former homeland, one person at a time. 'The world would be a better place without Kim Jong-il, of course. But the most important thing is not him, it's the people he rules.' Kim pays ten freelance journalists inside North Korea – including a university professor, a teacher and at least two soldiers – a retainer of about $100 a month to file reports. FNKR provides them with small digital recorders for recording interviews and mobile phones with signals that work across the Chinese border, since Pyongyang's fledgling mobile-phone system was imported from Egypt (in a joint venture with Pyongyang) and is incompatible with the South Korean network.

Why Chinese phones? Because it's difficult for the North Koreans to monitor calls, explains Martyn Williams of IDG. 'On the domestic network it's relatively easy for the security services to listen in on calls – the mobile operator allows them to do so – but by using a Chinese network the monitoring would have to be done on Chinese soil, and that is probably politically impossible.' But he adds that the North's security services may have detection units along the border that try to triangulate the source of cell phone signals and catch people using phones.

The recordings are spirited across the Chinese border and transported back to Seoul via a network of spies. The results detonate on air during the FNKR programme 'Voices of the People', where the raw views of the North's citizens are broadcast back into their own country, electronically distorted. Kim Jong-il's wealth comes from 'the sweat and blood of the people', says one. Another vows to protest government policies.

The aim of the clandestine recordings is simple, says Kim: changing the consciousness of ordinary North Koreans for the day when Kim Jong-il steps down. 'When power moved from Kim Il-sung [father of the nation] to Kim Jong-il, it was considered a natural development. But people know far more about the outside world now and they're more sceptical of the leadership, so anything could happen.'

Another defector, Choi Jin I, runs six reporters and four assistants inside North Korea, and at least three more across the border in China, from his cramped office in Seoul. Over the last three years, the reporters have filmed more than 200 hours of video footage, which is smuggled out on tiny SD memory cards and onto television screens in South Korea, Japan and much of the rest of the world. Stills from the reporting are printed in the bi-monthly magazine *Rimjingang*, published in Hangul and Japanese. 'The thing is, digital media has completely transformed how we gather information,' says Jiro Ishimaru, chief editor of *Rimjingang* in Japan. 'A decade ago if you gave a North Korean a video camera they wouldn't know what it was. Now, cameras are small and anyone can use them.'

The footage is secretly filmed, copied and even edited inside North Korea, he explains. 'People have their own PCs. It's printer drivers that are banned, to stop distribution.' He says that mobile phones can now be used to send texts and possibly more. 'We're very close to being able to send photos.'

The dangers of such clandestine reporting are obvious: *Rimjingang*'s journalists live in fear of being discovered. In 2007, many of Free North Korea Radio's original team of stringers were caught and tried as spies, then sent to labour camps or perhaps executed. 'We don't know what happened to them exactly,' says Kim, adding that their capture 'devastated' him.

Web-based publishers and blogs are also helping to inform our picture of life inside the North. NK News, run by Washington-based researcher Tad Farrell, aggregates articles, opinion pieces and travelogues from the

uriminzokkiri

@uriminzok PYONGYANG

http://www.uriminzokkiri.com

 ✔ Following 📋 🔁   ☰

Timeline   Favorites   Following   Followers   Lists ▾

uriminzok uriminzokkiri
우리 인민의 철천치 원쑤 김정일 력도와 아들 김정은을 몰
새 세상을 만들자!
8 Jan

uriminzok uriminzokkiri
조선인민군대여! 인민군들을 먹일 돈으로 핵과 미싸일 개발
억 딸라를 랑비한 김정일 력도에게 총부리를 겨누자
8 Jan

uriminzok uriminzokkiri
로망난 김정일과 폭악한 새끼 돼지 김정은을 한 칼에 처단
리도 남녘의 인민들처럼 이밥에 고깃국을 먹으면서 행복ㅎ
보자
8 Jan

uriminzok uriminzokkiri
300만 인민들이 굶어죽고 얼어죽었는데 초호화별장에서 처
과 난잡한 술파티를 벌이고 있는 김정일을 처단하자
8 Jan

uriminzok uriminzokkiri
민족의 리익부터 생각한다면 우리의 중대제안을 받아들여
http://tinyurl.com/3ysfsvl
7 Jan

uriminzok uriminzokkiri
남측은 우리의 중대제안에 성실히 응해나서야 한다

countryside outside the Potemkin Village of Pyongyang [http://www.nk-news.net/index.php]. It gets about 500 hits a day and claims to have been the first outlet to break the news that Pyongyang's famous traffic police girls had been retired. News website Daily NK [http://www.dailynk.com/english/] publishes translated propaganda and has been sourcing stories from stringers and defectors since 2004, with an undisclosed number of correspondents working along the border with China. It also uses about ten translators (some working voluntarily) to bring the latest developments in Korea, China and Japan.

Curtis Melvin, a doctoral student at George Mason University in the US, works with anonymous collaborators to build up a Google Earth profile of the isolated backwater on nkeconwatch.com. Melvin has identified prison camps, military facilities and mass graves from the famine in the 1990s that killed at least 2 million people. 'Its Wikipedia approach to spying shows how Soviet-style secrecy is facing a new challenge from the internet's power to unite a disparate community of busybodies,' concluded the *Wall Street Journal*.

The country's citizens are being primed for political change

Daily NK has brought details to the sketchy rumours surrounding Kim Jong-un's rise, and added much needed colour to the profile of Kim Jong-il's youngest son and likely heir. Florid official propaganda published on the website last year welcomed him as 'the number-one guard of [Kim Jong-il]', joining his father in wind and rain on his official visits. Kim Senior was quoted as calling his son 'a genius of geniuses' in propaganda distributed to party cadres. 'There is nobody on the planet who can defeat him in terms of faith, will and courage.' The excessive language is a sign, according to the website, that the country's citizens are being primed for political change.

Money is a headache for all these outlets. 'It's a major struggle,' admits Ishimaru of *Rimjingang*, which sells its footage to the big television stations, especially in Japan, where 3 to 4m yen for an exclusive is not uncommon. 'Our policy is to maintain strict editorial independence,' he explains. 'For the networks, the advantage is that there is little or no risk to them.' NK News

North Korea's official Twitter account, 9 January 2011
Credit: Lee Jae Won/Reuters

runs on a tiny budget of perhaps $1,000 a year, but is searching for more regular support. Daily NK relies on fundraisers, donations and subscriptions, says chief editor Park In Ho, though he is coy about the details.

The spate of new outlets has added detail to what we know about the North, but how reliable are they? One problem, says Lloyd Parry, is that 'they all have obvious agendas' – to topple the Kim regime. Daily NK, for example, was reportedly intensely disliked by the liberal Roh Moo Hyun administration, which viewed its anti-Pyongyang line as disruptive to its 'Sunshine' policy of slow, incremental détente initiated in the 1990s. (Roh was subsequently replaced by the conservative President Lee Myung Bak, who still rules.) But Lloyd Parry accepts that websites and blogs increasingly supplement the knowledge of reporters working the North Korea beat.

'The science of Pyongyang-ology largely depends on the scouring of official propaganda, and looking at photos,' he notes. 'Even if you had time to immerse yourself in all that, it's difficult to get hold of the material. [The new media means] it's easier to be a Pyongyang-ologist, to access information that used to be the preserve of a few experts.' He cites the example of a *Times* reader who recently analysed propaganda photos of Kim Jong-il after his stroke in 2008 and described how they were faked in the newspaper's comments section.

Much of the money that keeps Free North Korea Radio on air comes from the US State Department – at no cost to editorial independence, insists Kim. 'I'm asked about interference a lot, but it's not an issue. There has been just one clash. We ran a programme carrying testimony by defectors who spoke of their treatment – being beaten by guards at the Chinese border and so on. One defector said he was going to shoot Kim Jong-il. The Americans told us to delete that programme or they wouldn't pay.'

NK News shuns reporting on the Chinese military for fear of retaliation. 'We know what the People's Liberation Army does in many cases as far as it relates to North Korea, especially when it involves physical activities, troop movements, contemplations of future policy, etc.,' says Park In Ho by email. 'But we don't want to endanger our reporters and know that China has the power to arrest them at any time and also regards the military as a state secret of some seriousness.'

Could the new media eventually replace print or broadcast television? Tad Farrell doubts it. 'I don't agree that old media is in decline, because people are essentially using NK News as a portal for old media's online presence – and, I hope, for our own content from time to time as well.' The strength of online outlets is their ability to stretch the limits of reporting, says Park. 'Traditional print media are restricted by pages, and television is restricted by time, but we are restricted by nothing. We can write about anything, in as great a quantity as we want.' But he warns that some web-based sources are dragging down the quality and reputation of web-based media. 'While the Daily NK emphasises its opinion as it relates to the facts, some other internet news media don't always deal only with the facts.'

Ishimaru believes his organisation plays a niche role – for now. 'They just don't have people like us working in the big Japanese television stations. In that sense, we're unique and very useful to them.' NK News has perhaps the clearest remit of all. 'Before the regime changes, our role is to report the news from inside North Korea. Other media outlets read what we write, and if they ask us for anything, we let them know what they want to know,' explains Park In Ho. When the regime falls, his team plans to expand to report the news and views of ordinary North Koreans. 'The South Korean people's voice is already well represented.' The job, he says, is 'making sure the voices of the North Korean people can be heard'. ❐

©David McNeill
40(1): 125/131
DOI: 10.1177/0306422011399694
www.indexoncensorship.org

David McNeill writes for the *Independent*, the *Irish Times* and the *Chronicle of Higher Education*.
He teaches a course on the media at Sophia University in Tokyo

Virtual community

Saaed Valadbaygi, a young Iranian activist in exile, describes the impact of Web 2.0 on his generation – both inside and outside the country

Saeed Valadbaygi, 28, left Iran at the end of 2009 and was granted asylum in Canada. With more than ten years' experience of activism and blogging, he was a main source for international news in the aftermath of the elections. He continues to provide up-to-date reports on Iran to facilitate accurate analysis.

A very small percentage of those online are in Iran, yet some two million in the diaspora are actively connected. If we look at all the [political] movements, many of the key players have now left the country. That generation of activists was formed over two decades as life became more and more challenging. We would need another two decades to develop this again. In Iran, there is more newsworthy activity, but it is not accessible online. Here [outside Iran], there is less activity, but it's all online because there is freedom of expression. This opportunity has established stronger links inside and outside Iran. A dialogue has opened between people through the internet.

Looking back, with the political developments of 2 Khordad [Mohamed Khatami's 1997 landslide election victory] and 18 Tir [attack on student dormitories in 1999 that marked a turning point], the ground was ripe for activity. Communities were formed as everyone established themselves online, from famous photographers to the student movement and human rights groups. The internet became an essential tool and Iran ranked third after the United States and China in the size of its blogging community, with the Persian language the second most popular in the entire blogosphere. There were only two or three companies webhosting and internet service providers were controlled by the government. But people had blogrolls, discovered each other and communicated, first by chat through Yahoo! Messenger then weblogs and then email.

Before Google, your Yahoo! Messenger ID was crucial. People knew theirs like [their] phone number. The atmosphere has always been one of clandestine identities.

When I came to Canada, my use of the internet changed. [In Iran], I needed to know the best anti-filter software and back-up tools for not losing my work. Security from government spies is an issue for everyone in Iran, regardless if they are an activist. Now, finally, I am able to use [the internet] to its true potential.

The western media played an important role in establishing the net in Iran, as it was advertising computers on satellite radio and television stations that created popular awareness. At the same time, a group of fundamentalists campaigned against the use of computers. [President] Ahmadinejad's camp can be included among them, as well as various clerics, parliamentary representatives and even university deans and professors. The internet was a phenomenon and educating oneself was key. Once the culture of a phenomenon penetrates, it generates a fixation in people. This exploded in the heat of 2009. It took ten years for the culture and the tools to match it to integrate. First people acquired the hardware, then the software, and taught themselves with the tools before understanding the culture. Now we have seen a first generation of web users and the gap has been closed for experienced users like activists and bloggers, who learned with Web 1.0 and are now challenging themselves with Web 2.0. Twitter and Facebook and YouTube are all in place, but for the mainstream public there are still gaps.

Until June 2009, the people communicating from outside Iran were journalists and activists. I remember my first contact with the outside world when I was 15 or 16. We blindly followed anyone who was in touch. As the internet culture became familiar, I created my blog. After the election, YouTube was heavily filtered, so I used Facebook for uploading films and footage. YouTube is too slow in Iran, so Facebook was good for sharing videos. You could present an issue, your voice and material together. We quickly set up workshops on blogging, Facebook and tweeting, so more people could learn. This helped everything mushroom. At the time, the government was unaware of the impact of Facebook, but after the elections they began blocking the site.

Before June 2009, I had around 200 'friends'. This quickly became 100,000 after the live blogging we did. That was while I was still in Iran. After I left, we started the website Street Journalist [http://www.astreetjournalist.com]. During last year's Ashura [religious festival], we were the only source of live news in two languages, with minute-by-minute coverage, as well as live blogging with videos. This was a first in the history of Iranian web use, so the site had more than 14 million hits. Small things are happening. They have tried to hack the site, but we have made adjustments. The cyber army [hackers believed to be supported by the Iranian Revolutionary Guard] is more concerned with hacking sites to stop the interest generated than with individual people. That's left to the Ministry of Intelligence.

It's very difficult for people in Iran to keep up with the technology to combat the filters and deal with the slow servers. The servers in the internet cafes are faster, but you can't access the sites you want there, though technically they are more efficient and you are more protected in that you can send things without revealing your ISP. To upload five minutes of footage on YouTube could take 50 minutes at home. We use proxies through alternative domains, so the person in Iran is in effect uploading the video via our computers outside the country. There is no them without us – nor us without them.

In this potent climate, many new working relationships were formed and filled gaps in our previous endeavours. We suddenly had translators in different countries and were able to correspond with the media of each country in their language. When I was in Iran, my readership was English speaking and I wanted to write in English to communicate with the outside world. That has changed now. We created Street Journalist for that, but the 70,000 people linked to my various Facebook pages are mostly in Iran and I now mostly post in Persian. We strive to be independent of political groups, to be a people's media with

no restrictions. We have to be ahead with our interests and represent the many initiatives and movements occurring in Iran. Rather than accumulate numbers, I am trying to create democracy within our online discussions. You'll see fewer antagonistic attacks on this forum and most of the individuals expressing themselves are writing from Iran. A community has arisen. They communicate on the page and also by email.

The exile community is very relevant and represents the Iranian middle-class demographic well. Its members are organically linked and validate the struggle. It's as one body, though we are not geographically close. Non-Iranian participation and support too has been unbelievable. It was very surprising to Iranians in Iran that hearts elsewhere in the world beat for them, partly because of the bleak perception that people had of Iranians because of ostracism from the international community that had damaged the culture. Iranians felt they were closed off from the rest of the world. The Green movement introduced our culture to the international community – more than a million people protesting silently, walking side by side. ❐

Saeed Valadbaygi was talking to Negar Esfandiary

©Saeed Valadbaygi
40(1): 133/137
DOI: 10.1177/0306422011399705
www.indexoncensorship.org

139

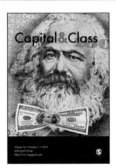

BLOG ON

As Saudi Arabia brings the internet under tighter control, **Ashraf Khalil** reports on one of the most active blogospheres in the region

Last September, Abdul Rahman al Hazaa appeared on the al Arabiya satellite news channel to talk about his government's new electronic media law. A spokesman for the Saudi Ministry of Culture and Information, al Hazaa explained that the burgeoning online publishing world required responsible monitoring and governance, and that all locally produced internet content would now be subject to the same rules and regulations as the country's heavily restricted print media.

Saudi's thriving blogosphere speculated that all bloggers would now be forced to register with the government. Al Hazaa's last name briefly became its own twitter hashtag category. 'Everybody went crazy,' said one Saudi blogger. Within a day, al Hazaa was forced to speak publicly again. This time he made it clear that Saudi's bloggers would not be required to seek government licences: the new restrictions would only apply to dedicated electronic news sites.

'We are not intending to license [blogs]. There are so many we cannot control them,' Al Hazaa said. 'If I shut one [blog] down, it would just pop up the next day under a new name.' Instead, he stated that bloggers would be 'encouraged' to register with the government, which also drew a fairly caustic response.

'Those who optionally register their blogs and information with the Ministry of Information, as they say, should also report their shower times to the Ministry of Water,' tweeted Fouad al Farhan, one of the most high-profile online activists [http://www.alfarhan.org].

At the time, many Saudi bloggers pointed to the incident as proof of their growing confidence. When the law was passed in January, bloggers were not required to register, as promised, but encouraged to do so voluntarily. Websites designated as 'electronic newspapers' will be subject to the new regulations and their editors-in-chief have to be approved by the government. The new regulations will also apply to multimedia websites, online advertisements, text messaging and mobile phone services, as well as 'any type of online publications that the ministry might find fit to add'

There are grave concerns about the impact of the legislation on freedom of expression in Saudi, and some international free speech groups believe that the question of registration for bloggers is irrelevant: they will still be liable to prosecution under the new legislation. According to Ahmed al Omran, the 26-year-old author of the popular SaudiJeans blog [http://saudijeans.org], the nation's bloggers are now waiting to see whether the new law will serve as a platform for further moves against them. One blogger commented: 'The kind of enthusiasm and energy the Ministry of Culture has put into this dumb idea is amazing. I only wish they would put this effort into something more useful.'

Saudi Arabia is widely regarded as the second most active blogging community in the Arab world – behind only Egypt, which has a population more than three times its size. Bloggers voiced their support for the protests in Egypt, despite King Abdullah's condemnation of the uprising. They also expressed their disapproval when Tunisia's ousted leader Ben Ali took refuge in Saudi Arabia in January.

Ahmed al Omran, who is currently studying journalism at Columbia University in New York City, explains that the social dynamics of the kingdom make it fertile ground for a new generation of tech-savvy youths seeking new forms of expression. 'You have a very young population, and this is the natural realm for them to express themselves. And let's be realistic, the newspapers in the country do not really represent the people.'

Blogs are filling the void left by Saudi's tame print media: they range from personal journals to highly politicised forums that seek to shine a light on social iniquities in Saudi society and include a significant number of

Blogger 'Saudi Jeans' in Riyadh, October 2006
Credit: Sultan al Fahed/Reuters

female bloggers. 'You have a lot of intelligent college-educated women who are basically unemployed,' al Omran says. 'The internet offers them this great space where they can say whatever they want without getting punished.'

Not every female Saudi blogger is campaigning for gender equality, but some of the most prominent blogs such as Saudi Amber [http://saudiamber. blogspot.com] and the Saudiwoman blog do overtly address such topics. Last November, a religious ruling banning women from working as department store cashiers was widely decried and openly mocked on a multitude of online forums.

'When I first started [in February 2008] I didn't know any Saudi women writing about the topic I was dealing with,' says Eman al Nafjan, the author of the Saudiwoman blog [http://saudiwoman.wordpress.com]. She focuses mainly on social issues such as women's rights, child brides and the Saudi educational system, as well as whimsical posts such as the video of 'Burka Woman' – a spoof of the Roy Orbison classic 'Pretty Woman'.

Online activity, and blogging in particular, mushroomed in Saudi from 2006. The authorities were initially a little slow to impose restrictions on the country's online community, despite the cultural taboos. 'There are a lot of vague red lines. You don't know until you're actually crossed them,' says Louai Kofiah, a 26-year-old Jeddah resident and writer of the Haphazard blog [http://zlouk.blogspot.com].

In December 2007, authorities arrested Fouad al Farhan, one of the kingdom's most experienced and high-profile bloggers and online activists. Bloggers believe he was arrested for writing about the case of several human rights activists who had been secretly detained. His posts included an emotional video interview with one of the activists' mothers. He spent four months in prison before being released, and became the subject of an international pressure campaign. Al Omran of the Saudi Jeans blog said the government was surprised by the scope and intensity of the 'Free Fouad' campaign.

'It made it very difficult for the government to do that again,' he says. 'The international attention it received made them realise that they just can't do that anymore.'

Despite the successful mobilisation on al Farhan's behalf, the detention did succeed in sending a chill through the local blogosphere. Al Farhan remains active, but he has rarely discussed what happened to him during his months in detention, according to a friend. He politely declined to be interviewed for this article.

One blogger, who requested anonymity, said officials from the Saudi government have recently tried a new tactic – pressuring family members. 'Last year, the authorities went to my family and told them they were not happy with my writing,' the blogger says.

Al Omran has noticed that those who write in English, like himself, seem to be given greater leeway to tackle controversial and unpopular subjects: 'They think I won't have the same influence within the country,' he says.

On the other hand, the government's decision to block the Twitter pages of problematic bloggers or activists in 2009 reveals a quaint misconception of how the internet works: it doesn't actually stop anyone from tweeting since they can still access their account from a mobile phone. 'They're not very smart sometimes,' says one blogger.

Despite the roadblocks, many bloggers feel their community has passed a point of no return and can even pressure the government for specific reforms. Louai Kofiah, author of the Haphazard blog, points to a recent online campaign concerning Samar al Badawi, a divorced Saudi woman who was jailed in Jeddah for 'disobeying her father'. She was released after seven months in late October. 'They had to release her,' he says. 'It was a turning point for a lot of people who were sceptical of the power of online pressure.'

In the aftermath of the al Farhan arrest, some Saudi bloggers freely admit that they practise self-censorship in order to avoid a similar fate. 'I will write about people who practise free speech, but I don't personally fully practise free speech,' says al Nafjan, a married mother of three and a post-graduate student in Riyadh. She said she is often awed by the freedom and boldness of some of her Egyptian blogging counterparts. 'Some of them are absolutely fearless.'

In comparison, al Nafjan says that the Saudi blog contingent are still tiptoeing around some of the country's red lines – especially anything regard-ing the Saudi royal family. She cites one prime example from 2010 of this self-censorship at work: the recent murder trial of a Saudi prince in the UK. Prince Saud Abdulaziz bin Nasser al Saud was sentenced to life in prison last October for killing his longtime manservant in a London hotel. Even more damaging, from a Saudi cultural perspective, was the extensive evidence pointing to a homosexual relationship between the prince and his victim.

The salacious details of the trial dominated the British press, but were ignored by the Saudi media and dealt with very carefully by Saudi bloggers and tweeters. 'We would re-tweet things or post links to articles about it, but we didn't really talk about it or write original things,' al Nafjan says.

The biggest red line, she believes, is who will succeed 86-year-old King Abdullah and the current generation of elderly brothers and half-brothers. 'That's absolutely off limits. Nobody is to talk about it even though every-body is thinking about it.' How far Saudi's bloggers will feel able to push the boundaries in the wake of the new regulations will be the next test for a vibrant community. ❐

©Ashraf Khalil
40(1): 141/145
DOI: 10.1177/0306422011399839
www.indexoncensorship.org

Ashraf Khalil is Index on Censorship's Middle East regional editor. He is based in Cairo and writes regularly for *The Times*, *Wall Street Journal* and *Rolling Stone* magazine, Middle East edition

NARCO TALES

Bloggers and citizen journalists are telling the stories that the mainstream Mexican media no longer dares to report, says **Ana Arana**

It was a week before Christmas 2010. The killers were brazen. The street security cameras show one of them, a hooded figure, crossing the street in pursuit of Marisela Escobedo, a businesswoman turned anti-crime crusader. The video shows the assailant shooting her in the head as she clings to the doors of the palatial local government house in downtown Chihuahua. For ten days, Escobedo had held vigil in front of the government house to protest the lack of justice following the murder of her 16 year old daughter Rubi Marisol Escobedo, whose body was found burned and dismembered. Escobedo did not tire until Sergio Rafael Barraza Bocanegra, her daughter's former boyfriend, faced trial for the murder. The Chihuahua justice system exonerated him for lack of evidence. Escobedo did not give up and managed to get the ruling reversed. Her murder scandalised all of Mexico, a feat in a country where the drug war has claimed 30,000 victims in four years, with increasing acts of violence and mayhem.

After Escobedo's death, the most popular hashtag on Twitter to protest against the government was #mariselaescobedo. It's one of the most recent cases of Mexican citizens, especially the young, using social media networks

A man walks by a banner celebrating the death of Gulf Cartel gang leader Ezequiel Cárdenas Guillén ('Tony Tormenta'), killed on 5 November 2010, Monterrey, Mexico
Credit: Tomas Bravo/Reuters

to express their indignation at the current cycle of violence and the drug war. The debate against President Felipe Calderon's drug war has various hashtags in Twitter, all created by unhappy voters, including #FelipeCalderon, #narco, #Reynosa and #politicosmex.

For the past three years, bloggers, tweeters and Facebook users in many provincial Mexican cities have been taking on the role of the traditional news media and writing about the drug war as citizen journalists. According to the Fundación Mexicana de Periodismo de Investigación (MEPI), in at least 47 per cent of Mexico's territory the traditional media is only reporting one in ten stories related to the drug war. The Fundacion, an organisation dedicated to investigative journalism, reviewed leading newspapers in 11 Mexican states for the first six months of 2010.

The most cited blog in recent months is Blog del Narco [www.blogdelnarco.com], which carries all the latest news about drug-related incidents, submitted by readers. According to an Associated Press story last year, it was started by an internet security university student in 2010. The blog went national in July after posting a video showing the murder of a policeman by masked gunmen. Before his murder, the policeman was filmed claiming that a local prison warden was arming prisoners and releasing them at night to commit crimes. Four reporters covering the story were kidnapped by traffickers and only freed after local television stations aired the video.

The fame of the blog has created more citizen reporters who are putting their lives at risk. 'MexicanFatBoy1' is the online handle of a citizen who filmed federal troops on 5 November, as they unleashed a heavy attack against the late leader of the Gulf Cartel, Ezequiel Cárdenas Guillén, or 'Tony Tormenta', in the border town of Matamoros, Tamaulipas. No journalists were able to get close to the three-hour shoot-out, which included 600 Mexican Navy troops, helicopters and armoured cars. When he posted the video on YouTube it received more than 296,000 hits. It was used by every major Mexican and international television station. In an interview with the Mexico City daily *La Razon*, 'MexicanFatBoy1' ruefully admitted that he had not realised that the battle involved a top drug leader. 'I don't want the narcos to think I am filming them,' he said. 'I was just trying to show that there are shoot-outs in Matamoros, and it is not as calm as the media wants us to believe.'

Javier Oliva, a researcher at the Universidad Nacional Autonoma de Mexico UNAM, believes that citizen journalists put their lives at risk without an understanding of the dangers. He also believes that some of the citizen reporters also relish 'the reality show' aspect inherent in doing this work.

Perhaps because of this criticism, a student blogger at Tecnologico de Monterrey, who was the first to witness shootings on campus last year, found it necessary to defend her blog and her writing [http://m1zar.blogspot.com/]. She had been the first to describe an army shoot-out that left two students dead. The case was highly controversial, as the army claimed that the students were narco hitmen. 'Why did I write the blog?' she asks. 'First, because it was therapeutic, I won't deny it … the Tec made us take a test the next morning, when just a few hours earlier two students had been killed. When I went past the door, I could see the wall had been painted, the floor had been recently washed and I thought it was an insult to my intelligence and to their memory that we were being forced to act as if nothing had happened.'

There is a growing concern that drug gangs have penetrated social networks. Sergio Octavio Contreras, an analyst who works with the magazine *Etcétera*, believes that the drug trafficking sub-culture has entered every sector of Mexican life: 'They are now using the internet as a platform that promotes their freedom of expression, ideology and social building.' In the past, drug traffickers used home videos to spread their message, he says: 'But with the arrival of the internet and since the government unleashed the war on drugs, the use of the web by drug traffickers and the spread of their ideology has multiplied.'

So long as the traffickers continue to intimidate the mainstream media, with threats and tacit accords, the internet will remain a vital conduit for information on the drug war. As the Blog del Narco publisher has said: 'We publish everything, and if we don't, people get angry.' ❏

©Ana Arana
40(1): 146/149
DOI: 10.1177/0306422011399687
www.indexoncensorship.org

Ana Arana is the director of the Fundación Mexicana de Periodismo de Investigación (MEPI), an investigative journalism project in Mexico that works on regional projects with US, Mexican and Central American media. She is Index on Censorship's regional editor in Mexico

SPRING CHILL

After a short-lived taste of online freedom, Vietnam's bloggers continue to be the victims of a government crackdown. **Ben Bland** reports

After her husband, a prominent Vietnamese legal activist, was arrested and charged with 'spreading propaganda against the state' in November, Nguyen Thi Duong Ha found that access to her email account had been blocked. A lawyer herself, Ms Ha was acting as defence counsel for her husband, Cu Huy Ha Vu – a difficult job not made easier by the interference with her personal communications.

It is difficult to prove that this or any other cyber attack was government led – the secret police who proliferate in authoritarian states such as Vietnam do not generally forewarn their victims nor own up to their activities afterward. But political dissidents, bloggers and other government critics have increasingly found themselves the targets of electronic counter-measures over the last two years, while a growing number of websites, including the social network Facebook, have been blocked.

The electronic repression has been followed by arrests and prosecutions: a number of bloggers have been jailed on political charges or on other grounds that human rights activists believe are trumped up. Many democracy campaigners have long argued that the rapid rise of the internet and mobile phones would empower people to take on authoritarian governments that have held a grip on power and information for too long. Cheap electronic communications have doubtless given government critics in one-party states like Vietnam and China a greater voice and made it easier for them to organise.

But governments and security services have quickly learned to use the self-same online tools to track and crack down on these activists, adding a new weapon to their repressive armoury. The experience of Vietnam shows that rather than becoming a unilateral tool for democratisation, the internet is developing into another arena in which authoritarian states and their opponents clash.

The communist government in Vietnam tries to control information through ownership and censorship of the print and broadcast media. It also seeks to stifle dissent by accusing critics of spreading anti state propaganda, a catch-all political charge. But, as Vietnam's economy took off from the turn of the new millennium, access to computers and the internet began to accelerate at a swift pace and it became much harder for the government to stop the spread of information.

A 'Hanoi spring' of sorts ensued with Vietnamese citizens taking advantage of their new-found freedom to read more widely than ever before and talk online about politics, corruption and relations with China – topics long considered taboo in mainstream Vietnamese life. Thousands joined a vigorous online campaign against a controversial bauxite mining project in Vietnam's central highlands, concerned about the potential environmental damage and the involvement of a Chinese state-owned company. Many spoke out in support of Vietnam's claims over islands in the South China Sea that are the subject of a territorial dispute with China and several other neighbouring countries.

At the margins, several hundred previously isolated activists came together in 2006 to form a grouping known as Bloc 8406, named for the date of its founding, which launched a manifesto calling for democratic reforms in Vietnam. All of this internet-enabled activity did not go unnoticed by the government, which at first hit back through the legal system. The main backers of Bloc 8406, such as Nguyen Van Ly, a Catholic priest, were rounded up and jailed in 2007.

In late 2008, the government imposed new restrictions on bloggers, making it illegal for them to write about politics or use a pseudonym. But, Vietnamese activists say, what worried the government more than the hard-line democracy campaigners, who are small in number and

A Vietnamese closed-circuit court television shows the trial of Nguyen Van Ly, lower centre, 30 March 2007
Credit: Tran Van Minh/AP/PA

lack wider public support, was the way in which previously quiescent young Vietnamese people were starting to openly back boisterous online campaigns against government policy. Given the close links of some of Vietnam's communist leaders to their Chinese counterparts, the government appeared particularly concerned about the criticism of China that was at the heart of netizens' concerns about bauxite mining and the South China Sea islands.

From 2008 to 2010, several bloggers were arrested including Bui Thanh Hieu, who used the pen name Nguoi Buon Gio ('Wind Trader'), Nguyen Ngoc Nhu Quynh, who blogged as Me Nam ('Mother Mushroom') and Phan Thanh Hai, known as Anh Ba Saigon ('Saigon Brother Three'). With 17 bloggers or online activists still in prison, Vietnam is 'the world's second biggest prison for cyber-dissidents after China,' according to Reporters Without Borders. The campaign group ranked Vietnam 165th out of 178 countries in its latest global press freedom index.

Many activists had their internet access cut off and their email accounts interfered with. Taking a leaf out of China's book, at the end of 2009 government-controlled internet service providers started blocking Facebook, which had very rapidly attracted well over 1m users in Vietnam and was something of a rallying point for opposition to the bauxite project, as well as the websites of campaign groups such as Human Rights Watch. More worryingly – and also echoing similar actions in China – a growing number of email accounts, blogs and websites linked to government critics were attacked by hackers.

In March 2010, Google and McAfee, the anti-virus software provider, went public with claims that unidentified groups linked to the government were using malicious software to bring down websites and spy on tens of thousands of Vietnamese internet users. The government dismissed these allegations as 'groundless' and continues to insist that it protects freedom of speech in Vietnam and only arrests those who break the law.

In a large country of nearly 90m people, with 27m internet users, the government cannot hope to control everything that people do and say online. It is also aware that if it restricts the internet too aggressively, like Myanmar or North Korea, it risks damaging its impressive record of economic growth. Unlike the so-called Great Firewall of China, the Vietnamese block on Facebook and some other websites is relatively easy to circumvent.

But the changes to the law, arrests and cyber attacks have sent a clear message to Vietnamese internet users that they are being monitored and will not receive any extra leeway to speak out against the government just because they are conversing and connecting online. In the longer term, the ease of communicating and publishing on the internet is likely to lead to more political engagement and transparency, even in countries like Vietnam. However, this journey is likely to be long and drawn out, with many bumps in the road. ❐

©Ben Bland
40(1): 150/153
DOI: 10.1177/0306422011399688
www.indexoncensorship.org

Ben Bland is the Hanoi-based Vietnam correspondent for the *Financial Times*. Previously he worked as a freelance journalist covering the wider South-east Asian region from Singapore and Jakarta and as a business reporter for the *Daily Telegraph* in London. He blogs at http://theasiafile.blogspot.com/

social science **space**

Explore, share and shape the big issues in social science

Join researchers, scholarly associations, funders, think tanks, policy makers and government in this new online community for the social sciences.

- read **blog articles** from key figures
- discuss urgent concerns in the **forum**
- find and add **funding and job announcements**
- discover **free resources** including videos, reports and events listings.

Visit now to add your voice to the debate
www.socialsciencespace.com

Brought to you by **⑨SAGE**

LIVING
MEMORY

Dubravka Ugresic on cultural amnesia

Maureen Freely on Hrant Dink

Demonstrators hold signs reading 'We are all Armenians, we are all Hrant Dink', outside an Istanbul court where suspects are tried for the murder of the Agos editor, October 2007
Credit: Osman Orsal/Reuters

CHRONICLE OF A DEATH

The murder of journalist Hrant Dink marked a sea change in Turkey. **Maureen Freely** introduces an exclusive extract from the bestselling biography

Hrant Dink was the founder and editor-in-chief of the Turkish-Armenian newspaper *Agos* and one of Turkey's most prominent public intellectuals. It is largely thanks to his efforts that the 90-year taboo on public discussion of the darkest chapter in Turkey's history – the 1915 Armenian genocide – is now well and truly broken. Revered by those wishing for peaceful democratic change, he was feared and hated by the ultra-nationalists, who tried to silence him with a media hate campaign. Though Dink was prosecuted several times for 'insulting and denigrating Turkishness' and finally convicted, he refused to stop speaking. On 19 January 2007, he was gunned down in front of his newspaper office.

There is, alas, a long tradition of political assassinations in Turkey. Many have been killed after challenging state policy or the nation's strictly enforced official history. Only rarely have the perpetrators been made to pay for their crimes. Almost always, the public response to this spectacle of impunity has been terrified silence. But something changed with the death of Hrant Dink. More than a hundred thousand mourners from all religions, ethnic groups and backgrounds walked the five miles between his newspaper and the Armenian

church where he received his last rites, bearing placards emblazoned with the taboo-breaking words, 'We are all Armenians, we are all Hrant Dink.' Four years on, many in Turkey see this as the moment when the Turkish people found their courage, and came to understand the power of public conscience.

Tuba Çandar's biography of Dink has been on Turkey's bestseller lists since its publication last September, on what would have been Hrant Dink's 56th birthday. Drawn from hundreds of interviews, it is constructed like an oratorio, its voices weaving together a tapestry that is in every way unprecedented. The first half offers a harrowing portrait of Turkey's last remaining Armenians. The second half, which follows Dink's life as a political activist, gives us a glimpse of what it means – and what it costs – to fight for peaceful democratic change in Turkey.

It has been abundantly praised for celebrating Hrant Dink's life rather than his death. But its subversive potential has not gone unnoted. Its every sentence negates the official history that all Turkish children learn at school, which holds that the genocide is a fiction invented by the Armenian diaspora.

Protesters mark the anniversary of Hrant Dink's murder outside the Agos office, 19 January 2009
Credit: Osman Orsal/Reuters

It is a claim that a small but influential sector of the Turkish intelligentsia has been challenging with some passion for more than a decade. But in Tuba Çandar's biography, we leave behind the television studios and conference halls to discover what it really means to be an Armenian in a country that does not just deny the genocide, but brands all those who speak of it as traitors.

For almost a century, the golden rule has been silence. Many of those interviewed in this book are Turkish Armenians who have never before dared to speak in public. Their new confidence reflects a sea change in public culture and a genuine interest in their story. At the same time, these first-time speakers are only too aware that words are dangerous, leading to persecution, prosecution or death. In her introduction, Tuba Çandar speaks of the anguish many of her interviewees felt at the prospect of opening their lives to her, even though both she and her husband, the columnist Cengiz Çandar, were trusted friends of Hrant Dink and have, since his death, been closely involved with the international peace foundation set up by his family. Despite these credentials, Tuba Çandar was still a Turk from the secular elite and so an object of fear. It is a credit to her skill as an interviewer that she was able to persuade Hrant's friends and relations to speak with such candour.

The story they tell begins with Hrant's maternal grandfather. Drafted into an army chain gang in 1915, he returned home to discover that most of his family had been killed or deported. His second wife (Hrant's maternal grandmother) was also a survivor of the genocide, spared by a local land-owner who took her on as a servant and later sent her to an orphanage. Once married, the couple moved to the south-eastern city of Malatya, to join a small but tight-knit Armenian community in a neighbourhood known to others as the 'Hamam of the Infidels'. Hrant's paternal grandfather was the most educated (and so the most respected) man in this deeply impoverished community, but Hrant's father was a compulsive gambler. The family was thrown out of one house after another, and often the children had no food to eat. A move to Istanbul made matters worse, and Hrant's mother soon suffered a breakdown. Hrant and his brothers ran away, to be discovered days later in a fisherman's basket. The boys spent most of the rest of their childhood in an Istanbul orphanage run by Protestant Armenians, and it was thanks to the education Hrant received there that he was able to go to university. Later, with his brothers, he opened a bookstore that did well enough to give the family a secure and comfortable income.

By then, he was the veteran of the doomed student left, which rose in the late 1960s to be beaten down twice by military coups. He had done his military service, during which it was made clear to him that he was not considered a 'true' Turk. He had also served time in prison, accused, without basis, for having links with the Armenian terrorist group Asala, in the aftermath of the second coup in 1980. It was after another false claim circulated in the nationalist press in the 1990s, alleging that it was 'the Armenians' who were funding Kurdish separatist activities, that Hrant and a number of others decided their community needed to defend itself better, and to demand basic human rights. Hrant went on to found *Agos* in 1996. As its editor, he soon became a nationally known proponent of human rights, not just for his own people but for the whole country's persecuted minorities. In his frequent media appearances, he tried to persuade those listening that there was honour in acknowledging the darkest chapters of one's history, and hope in reconciliation. Always interested in family stories, and in the complex cultural mix that so often can be found beneath the veneer of pure Turkishness, he investigated the background of Atatürk's most famous and accomplished adoptive daughter, the aviator Sabiha Gökçen. She was, he claims, an Armenian orphan. It was not long after he had published this story in *Agos* that a virulent hate campaign was launched against him in the nationalist press. Then came the prosecutions, and the death threats.

The following excerpt is taken from one of the last chapters in Çandar's biography. It traces Hrant's increasing distress at being branded an enemy of the people, and his silent panic as the walls closed in on him. Most of its voices come either from Dink's immediate family (his wife Rakel, his son Arat, his daughters Delal and Sera, his brothers Hosrof and Yervant) or his 'second' family at *Agos*. These include writers, members of his staff, his lawyer Fethiye Çetin, and several prominent journalists and activists (Etyen Mahçupiyan, Rober Koptaş, Ali Bayramoğlu, and Ragıp Zarakolu). Woven into their recollections are excerpts from Dink's own writings.

As the chapter begins, Hrant has just heard that the Court of Appeals has confirmed a six-month sentence for insulting Turkishness. He had previously said he would leave the country if the courts found him guilty, but by the end of the chapter, he has decided to take the case to the European Court of Justice, and so in Turkey he stays. But the death threats continue. And now his anonymous attackers have begun to take an interest in his son.

Hrant Dink: For me the most unbearable thing has been the psychological torture I have endured alone. I see it sometimes in documentaries. The lions are going after a pack of animals but the pack has left one animal behind. The plan all along is to separate one animal from the pack and then descend on it en masse. I believe that they have isolated me and made me their target in much the same way. Anxiety is one aspect of psychological torture, and another is apprehension. You are cautious, and easily startled. I'm just like a pigeon ...

Arat Dink (his son): I knew that after the Court of Appeals ruling, my father was horribly upset, even indignant, but I had no idea he was worried about me also. In 2006 we had a robbery. It was Easter weekend. My wife Karolin had gone with our daughter Nora to my parents. We stayed the night there. On Sunday, we got news that our house had been robbed. We went straight over with my father. That was when I saw he was worried in some new way. 'Are you sure?' he asked the police. 'This might not really be a robbery.' He even asked, 'Did they leave a note?' At another point, he said, 'It's a good thing you stayed with us last night.' That day I could tell from the way my father looked at me that there was a possibility of a threat. It seems that around that time they'd sent a threatening letter to my father saying, 'We are going to kill your son and [journalist] Sarkis Seropyan.' That's why he feared the robbery might really be something else ...

Sarkis Seropyan (Agos editor): Hrant never spoke to me directly about the threats he was getting. Only once he showed me a letter in which there was a threat directed against Arat and me. 'They're obviously fake, but look, they're even giving their names and addresses these days,' he said. We read the letter together. If it hadn't named his son, he might not have given it so much importance. But that was what really upset him. 'What do they want with my family?' he said. The letter said that he would find Arat's body and mine near a gendarmerie on the outskirts of Ankara. The handwriting was terrible, and the paper was poor quality. At our next editorial conference, Hrant started asking, 'What shall I do? Shall I leave? Will you be able to carry on with *Agos?*'

Fethiye Çetin (lawyer): One day Hrant called me and said, 'I've received a threat in the post.' I asked him if he wanted me to complain to the courts. He said he didn't. He was beside himself. 'I don't care about the threats they made about me, but if they start threatening my family and those around me, that is another matter all together,' he kept insisting. Later he sent me the letter. 'Hrant Dink, we're going to silence you, your son, and Sarkis Seropyan so that you can never speak again. But first you are going to have to collect your son's body from a gendarmerie on the outskirts of Ankara.' That's what the letter said. But of course it was not possible to locate the person who had sent the letter.

Hrant Dink: My inbox and my hard drive were full of hate mail and threats. How many of these threats were real, how many were fantasies? The truth is that there is no chance I shall ever know. If it were just me, there wouldn't be a problem. All my life I've put myself on the line, lived on the edge of danger. Let me just say that one of these letters, sent from Bursa, alarmed me because it spoke of immediate danger. And let me add that – even though we turned the letter over to the Şişli prosecutor – the matter has not been resolved.

Ali Bayramoğlu (journalist): One day I had a phone call. I can no longer remember if it was [the journalist] Etyen [Mahçupiyan] or Hrant. They told me that Hrant had received another threatening letter. They'd discussed it amongst themselves and then they decided to tell me about it. I got up and went over to *Agos.* This was a letter from Bursa, signed by an Ahmet Demir. Ahmet Demir is a man who also uses the codename 'Green', by which I mean

Hrant Dink in his office in Istanbul, 10 October 2006
Credit: Fatih Saribas/Reuters

to say, this is not a joke. This brute had written, 'You are going to collect the bodies of your son and Seropyan from outside the gendarmerie.' Hrant was beside himself. Over and over again, he said, 'The threats against me don't matter. But what am I to do if it's about my child?' At this point I rang Hanefi Avcı. At that point he was the head of security in Edirne. When I'd told him what happened, he said, 'He should take this letter to the governor's office at once. He should ask for protection. But I don't think anything much can happen from this sort of letter.' After this we spoke for the first time about whether or not he should go abroad.

Ferhat Kentel (lecturer): We were at a Helsinki Citizens meeting [group dedicated to peace]. As we were leaving the hall, Hrant came up to a number of us and said, 'Listen friends, I'd like to talk to you about something. But I don't know how I can say it.' In a trembling voice he talked about the death threat. 'I get death threats all the time, but this time I just didn't know what to do,' he said. We all froze. After that Hrant went so far as to beg us not to mention this letter to anyone. Most particularly, he did not want his family to know. He wanted to hide his fear inside him. In wishing to keep his family and his children from knowing, he was really trying to protect them from fear.

Leda Mermer (production editor, Agos*):* During those last six months, it was as if he were caught in a vice. As if he were in prison. The volume of threats coming into *Agos* had gone way up, and he exploded with a curse, saying, 'Erase them.' Then one day he said, 'I'm thinking of the children.' He told me that he'd received a death threat against his son, but even as he was telling me this he was saying that he didn't want to scare Arat. 'We are going to execute your son on the Ankara road.' That was the sentence that turned him upside down. That day, for the first time, he uttered a sentence along the lines of 'Should I stay, or should I go?' He seemed unable to make up his mind.

Mayda Saris (culture editor, Agos*):* After that period when he'd walk up and down his room for hours in solitude, he slowly began to share his concerns with us. After all, the death threats came through the *Agos* computer, so we all knew about them. Then at our meetings he began to talk about requesting protection. We tried very hard to convince him, but he wouldn't listen. Summer had arrived, and he loved to go fishing. And he was thinking about how you can't go out fishing when you have protection. And on top of that, he probably didn't have much confidence in bodyguards ...

Necdet Koçtürk (friend): We went fishing in Kınalı all summer. For hours, he would sit next to me in silence. We two look alike. We are both fearless and enterprising men. But this had its drawbacks. There you were, cut from the same cloth, but he still would not share his troubles. Because he saw we were both feeling the same, he saw no point in sharing his problems or his worries. So, for example, I was very disturbed by these [Article] 301 trials [at the time of Hrant's murder, 301 was a controversial article of the Turkish penal code making it illegal to insult Turkishness. It has since been amended to insulting the Turkish state]. I was ready to go into those hearings with him, and I was steeling myself not to attack those cursed men, those Kerinçsiz people [Kemal Kerinçsiz, Turkish ultra-nationalist lawyer, who filed lawsuits against Hrant Dink]. And I'd told him so. But he never once gave me the dates of his hearings. Maybe because he thought I'd do something crazy. And I had my pride, I held back, I mean to say I didn't go into a panic, and maybe he thought this meant I didn't care, and so he didn't share his worries with me.

Hrant Dink: It's a hot day ... The waters are still. It's red snapper weather ... I'm lucky enough to have owned a rowboat for some time now, and I have a fishing rod, too. But please bear in mind that I'm no master of this sort of thing. I am insanely jealous of the way everyone else in this boat keeps pulling out these red snappers. Whereas for me it's a thousand to one chance. If I catch a red snapper, it has to attach itself to my line. And that's not enough, either, for there is the other feat of pulling it into the rowboat with the skimmer.

Up until now I have only managed to catch two red snappers of any size. It would be more accurate to say that I threw water over their faces. Though the first one got away because I panicked, I did manage to bring in the second.

'Red snappers shed tears when they're caught.' Or so our elders liked to say. After checking that my catch wasn't shedding tears, I threw it back into the bucket. Does that mean that I would have swung it back into the sea if I'd seen tears? And of course there were many tiny red snappers that I caught in my setline, and I never bothered to see if they were crying before throwing them back in.

You don't need much know-how to use a setline. You don't need bait or indeed anything. You just swing its rows of feathered hooks and see what bites. Whatever God gives.

But you know what God's like ... He doesn't give everything, and sometimes he swings his setline. Whatever his subjects give ... he pulls his line up. It's a treacherous game. Tossing these setlines like javelins all over the world, to let them sway so treacherously ... Catching so many tiny babies with those hooks ... All blameless, all innocent ... Some hungry, some ill ... All those red snappers ... Oh you poor little things. Why do you leave your tears behind for us? Why don't you ever look up at the heavens all together? Why don't you shed tears when you're pulled up to the heavens? Why don't you ever try to convert this ruthless hunter? Why didn't you shake yourselves free and come back to us?

Hosrof Dink (brother): We spent the summer of 2006 together at Kınalı. We went fishing all the time. On the days when he wasn't fishing, he'd always come by *Agos*, to ask if anything new had happened. He'd read through whatever messages had come to the computer. 'Erase these,' he'd say. 'More threats?' I'd ask. 'No, there's nothing,' he would reply. By now he wasn't telling me anything. We'd just fish together and play cards. We spent the whole summer like that.

Necdet Koçtürk (friend): Just at the end of the summer, we went to Saroz to go fishing. Then we went looking for a place to play cards. By chance, the place we found was just across from the MHP local headquarters [Nationalist Action Party, extreme right-wing nationalist party]. Hrant got very uneasy, and he even said, 'Let's not sit here.' And can you believe it, it was only then that I became aware of just how uneasy he'd become. That was when I really got worried. I took him by the arm and said, 'While I'm here with you no one will dare touch you.' He looked at me as if to say, are you joking? I had no idea what he'd been going through. Just once he brought up the idea of a bulletproof vest, asking, 'Do those things really work, do they really protect you?' And as a joke, I said, 'It wouldn't protect *you*, because they'll shoot you in the head.' Now why on earth would anyone say such a thing? How could anyone? But you see, I said just that ...

Yervant Dink: My brother and I talked about whether or not he should go abroad. This was around the time he told me the death threats had increased. We'd even got to the point of my saying, 'Why don't you just take your children and go to Belgium. You can stay with your little daughter.' It was in this room that we also talked about whether or not he and Etyen should buy bulletproof vests, and struggled together to make the right decision.

Etyen Mahçupyan (Agos *editor*): For a short while we both wore bulletproof vests ... There was a factory in Manisa; we even had them brought to us from there. But it was hard to get used to them so we stopped wearing them. Hrant didn't want a bodyguard either.

One day he talked to me about whether he should go or not; but he didn't want to go. He wasn't the sort of person who could live abroad. We talked about it for a very long time that day. 'I said, 'If there isn't a single question mark in your mind, then stay, but if you have the faintest doubt, leave at once.'

Hrant kept changing his mind about whether he should go or not. Whenever he told someone else not to worry, nothing was going to happen, he'd want to talk about it the moment we were alone. At one point, he had more or less decided he should leave. He had a meeting with his family. He brought it up with them. The next day he called me to tell me about the meeting and he said, 'We've decided to stay here, they want to live in the same place as I am.'

Hrant Dink: And then, you see, the threats began to increase. ... I was left by myself, all alone. I can't tell my son about all this, I can't talk to my family. I could only talk about this to one or two close friends. Then there was one threat I just couldn't bear, and I turned it over to the prosecutor.

In the end, I called my family together one evening. Without alarming them, I wanted to let them know what we would do if we had to make a decision whether or not to leave. 'Wherever you are, we are,' they said.

Rakel Dink (wife): I have no idea how much he shared with his brothers. During the last two years, when he came out to the island, he always had Orhan [also known as Hosrof, his Armenian name] with him. You could even say that he became his older brother's bodyguard during that last year. Levent, on the other hand, was at the White Man [the Dink brothers' bookshop], though he certainly shared in our anxieties. As for what they talked about, and how much, I have no idea whatsoever!

One day, we heard a gunshot somewhere near our house. I shall never forget the way Orhan panicked. He was full of anxiety and fear for his brother. He was always on edge. But so were we all ...

One day we invited Arat and Karolin to the house. We sat at the table in the kitchen. 'Look, children,' he began. 'It might be necessary for us to leave this country. Because of me, you may have to change your lives,' he said. Looking especially at Karolin, he said, 'My daughter, it could be hard for you to be so far away from your loved ones, from your family, but I would have a hard time living anywhere without you.' Then Karolin said something lovely. 'Father, wherever you are, I'll come. Don't you worry about me for a minute.' Then Hrant said, 'If necessary we can find a new way to live; we can leave and the children can go back and forth.' With that he brought the conversation to a close. Until the next time ...

Arat Dink: I didn't know there had been a death threat directed against me. My father never told me. It was, I think, at the beginning of the summer of 2006. One evening he invited us to the house, with Karolin. We were sitting around the kitchen table – Sera [Hrant's youngest daughter], my mother, my father, Karolin and me. We started talking about the possibility of leaving. If we went to Armenia, we would have the same sort of life, we agreed. As far as democracy is concerned, it's no different from here, we said. Then we

Arat Dink and Özlem Dalkıran at the 2008 Index on Censorship Freedom of Expression Awards
Credit: Karim Merie

considered going to Brussels, because Baydzar [Dink's daughter, also known as Delal] worked and lived there.

Father turned to me and asked, 'If we went to Brussels would you come too?' I said, 'You and Mother should go immediately.' It would make no sense for us to go, too. I had one or two semesters to do before finishing university. Sera wasn't enthusiastic either. She didn't want to leave her school. 'When we finish, we'll join you,' I said. We even spoke about what kind of work we could do there. But we did not reach any sort of decision; everything was left up in the air. When I insisted, 'But there's no point in my leaving,' my father said, 'You just go on thinking that.' After which I said, 'If they are getting to you by using my name, then it's because they are trying to scare you,' or something along those lines. This was not because I knew anything, it just came into my mind, it was my intuition talking.

In the end we left it to my father to decide. But we also told Baydzar to look for a larger house. She did look for a house for us. But my father never said, 'It's decided,' so nothing came of that either ... And also my father was going abroad a great deal to collect the prizes he was being awarded around then. These trips served to calm his nerves for a time. It seemed as if this allowed him to postpone the decision to leave.

There was something else interesting going on at this point that I found out about afterwards. In October 2006, my father took part in a panel discussion arranged by some students at Boğaziçi. At the time, the panel seemed unimportant, but when we look back, it's clear we must take it seriously. Because when he was answering the students' questions, for the first time he spoke openly about being threatened by the state, and this was the first time he went outside his family and his circle of friends to speak about it in public.

Hrant Dink: Until today I have not spoken about this nor have I written about it. Certainly I shall write about it one day soon, I shall describe what has been going on and why. Because this is what I have been through. I don't know if it is right for me to tell you this, but I am subject to an intimidation campaign that is coming from the depths of the state. Because these people themselves told me so.

I can jog your memories perhaps. Last year I put out a news story. In this news story, I offered the documentation to prove that Atatürk's adopted daughter, Sabiha Gökçen, was really an Armenian orphan, that he'd adopted her from an orphanage.

[The newspaper] *Hürriyet* made this headline news. After that all of Turkey was boiling. Everyone came after me. The general staff issued a statement, to the effect that the person who had published this news had done so to spread discord and threaten the unity and integrity of the nation. The next day I received an official summons and was told that I was going to be put in my place.

It was after that day that the ultra-nationalists went into action and came knocking on my door, and various columnists plucked my sentences one by one and started writing about me. And it was after that day that the prosecutions started and I was found guilty under [Article] 301, while still being prosecuted under the same article in other cases. To this day they have been trying to put me in my place ... I am going to talk about this in public one day soon and somewhere I shall write about it, I shall tell people.

Delal Dink (daughter, also known as Baydzar): During that last period, when the state was really bearing down on him, something odd was going on; because he was getting one award after another outside the country.

He was getting awards abroad, and then he'd come back to Turkey to be found guilty. Once Cemil Çiçek [then minister of justice, famous for incendiary ultra-nationalist remarks] said something strange. Something like: 'They shouldn't complain too much when they're always off collecting prizes.'

Comments like this really upset him, because what he wanted more than anything was for his country to understand him correctly. That's why he didn't let anyone in Turkey know how pleased he was to receive the Ayşe Zarakolu Prize [Turkish human rights prize]. Before this, when he won the Henri Namen Prize in Germany, he was very impressed by the red carpet, but in his talk, he insisted that his country wasn't a dark place, and then he reminded the European nations of their responsibilities ...

In November 2006, he went to Holland with my mother to collect the PEN Freedom of Expression Prize. When he saw journalists around him just as he was boarding the plane, he was very surprised. 'Just think how ironic,' he said to me. 'Guess what our boarding gate was – 301!'

Hosrof Dink: Then one day ... it was November by now. I was heading home late. I'm on the road. I get a phone call from my older brother. He'd never usually call me at that hour. 'Where are you?' he asked. 'I'm going home, shall I come to you instead?' I asked. There was a pause. 'No,' he said. Later it occurred to me that he'd probably wanted to talk to me that day. And also in November, this other thing happened: when my brother and Rakel were out of the country to collect another prize, two people turned up at their house. According to the janitor's statement, they were wearing masks. First they said they were police, and when the janitor got suspicious, they'd made a threat – 'Tell him that his days are numbered' – and left.

When my brother returned from Europe, the janitor told him what had happened. He'd told the janitor not to worry, and that quietened him down. I found out about this after they killed my brother. I said, 'You know, he never told me about any of this.' He didn't tell Arat he'd been threatened either. But I didn't get angry at him. We were in prison together when we were young. He knew my state of mind very well. He knew I would be on his case, that I would say, 'You're not the sort of person who can live alone. You have a family here that depends on you. If something happened to you, what would we do?' He knew I would put pressure on him to leave. ... He didn't tell our other brother either, after all. He didn't talk about this with anyone in the family.

Delal Dink: During those last days, every time he came to Europe, he would try to convince himself: 'This is not such a bad place, actually, we could live here, couldn't we?' And then he would wait for me and mother to give our opinions. When they went to Norway to collect the prize, both of them were very impressed with the country. When they stopped off at Brussels on their way back, they said, 'Let's find you a place of your own here. We could come and go.' So then I started looking for houses.

He'd said many times how much he wanted to stay in Turkey, after all, and he'd said it in writing, too, but he also wanted to live with his grandchildren, grow old with them. Even when we were talking about my moving to Brussels, he was uneasy. 'You could get married here and settle down, and then my grandchildren wouldn't know me.' To which I said, 'As if you know where you'll be living anyway,' and then his face grew dark, and he frowned and said, 'You're right about that too.'

Rober Koptaş (executive editor, Agos): At around this time, on the days when I stopped by *Agos*, I'd see him pacing up and down the corridor, muttering to himself. Once I heard him say, 'They're trying to corner me, but I'm not going to play their game!' He was livid, he couldn't sit still. I didn't know what he was angry about, but those were difficult times, it was clear from his every gesture. He seemed to be buckling under the pressure. He told me he had won a prize in Norway. He was happy about that but he was also bitter, because he was wondering if he was getting these prizes because of the anti-Turkish sentiment in Europe. He didn't act as if the prizes coming from Europe were an honour. I remember him saying, 'When I go there, I am going to give such and such a speech, and put them in their place ...' There were still two months to go before he collected the prize.

Ragıp Zarakolu (publisher): After the Court of Appeals ruling, Hrant talked to me too about whether or not to leave. But he didn't do it, he didn't go ... The last time Hrant and I met up was in December 2006. Because there was a new case against me and I had to go to the hearing, I'd not been able to use a ticket I'd bought to London. I was very upset about this. Hrant immediately arranged a new ticket and it was with the ticket he'd bought me that I was able to travel abroad. It was as if life was playing games with us. He didn't leave the country, but I did, with the ticket he'd bought me. And it was while I was abroad that I got the news he'd been shot.

Fethiye Çetin: The new year began badly for Hrant. Three days after the Court of Appeals ruling, they opened a new case against him for running an article in *Agos* about being called into the prosecutor's office to be inter-rogated after using the word 'genocide' in a statement he gave to Reuters. After which [the historian] Taner Akçam wrote an article in which he said, 'I use this word every day. So that means they should be prosecuting me, too.' Of course nothing of the sort happened.

After giving our deposition at the prosecutor's office on 5 January, we went with Taner back to *Agos*. We sat in Hrant's office and discussed what sort of a defence we would prepare for this new case they were making under Article 301. We also discussed the petition we were preparing for the European Court of Human Rights to protest the Court of Appeals ruling. As we were talking about what we would do and how, he suddenly began to describe how deep an anxiety he was suffering. He couldn't bear to look us in the face. He talked and talked. He said, '2007 is going to be a difficult year for me.'

This wasn't the Hrant we knew. Taner and I both told him he had to get away from this place for a while. 'Whoever I talk to, they tell me I should leave,' he said. But it was clear that he wasn't going to be able to go easily. We were going to have to force him. But you see, we didn't manage it. ❐

©Tuba Çandar
40(1): 157/173
DOI: 10.1177/0306422011399689
www.indexoncensorship.org

Maureen Freely is a writer, translator and professor at Warwick University. Her latest novel, *Enlightenment*, is published by Marion Boyars. **Tuba Çandar** is an author and former journalist. *Hrant* (Everest) is her third biography

THE LONDON BOOK FAIR®

40 YEARS

11 – 13 APRIL 2011
EARLS COURT, LONDON

Making words go further

The London Book Fair is the global marketplace for rights negotiation and the sale and distribution of content across print, audio, TV, Film and digital channels.

The London Book Fair offers you the opportunity to meet with over **23,000 publishing professionals** from **112 countries*** over **3 days** at a key time in the publishing calendar.

Be a part of The London Book Fair 2011
Find out more at www.londonbookfair.co.uk/ioc

*Official LBF 2009 audited figures

RUSSIA
MARKET FOCUS 2011

SELECTIVE MEMORIES

In Croatia, Yugoslavia is a dirty word and libraries purged of communist literature. **Dubravka Ugresic** considers the politics of cultural amnesia

A ten-year-old friend of mine recently spent his Easter holidays with me in Amsterdam. I took him to the Anne Frank Museum. He had never heard of Anne Frank. I tried to recall whether I had known who Anne Frank was when I was his age. And then my childhood diary came to mind. I had written to an imaginary friend in that diary, and my imaginary friend's name was – Anne Frank.

Last year I was very fortunate: I spent two months teaching students of comparative literature at a German university. Several spoke a number of languages fluently; they were young and already remarkably worldly, a little international group. Some of them were also socially privileged diplobrats.

I was free to speak on whatever I liked. At one point I realised that out of a natural desire to help the students follow me I was turning my lectures into a list of footnotes. My students knew who Lacan, Derrida and Žižek were, but the number of books they had read was astonishingly small. I would mention a name, such as Ceszlaw Milosz, but my students did not know of Ceszlaw Milosz. I would give them a word such as samizdat, but my students did not know what a samizdat was. This is all entirely understandable, I thought,

What is remembered: souvenirs of former Yugoslavia's president Josip Broz Tito (1892–1980) for sale in downtown Sarajevo, May 2009
Credit: Eddie Gerald/Laif/Camera Press

and I did what I could to explain: in some former communist countries manuscripts were distributed clandestinely, in copies typed up on a typewriter, I said. Then I realised that it was more than I could do to explain what carbon paper was and what copies were, simply because I was not able to explain – the typewriter! Typewriters now dwell in the limbo of oblivion: they haven't yet surfaced in museums, yet they can no longer be found in stores. Of course they can still be seen in movies …

The East European culture that had been created under communism dwells in a similar limbo of oblivion. This was an intriguing culture and the shared ideological landscape gave it a certain consistency – the landscape of communism. It was a fact that the finest part of that culture was born of its defiance of communism, split into the 'official' and the 'underground' sides. Aspects of that cultural landscape are a part of many of us. Among us there are many who remember the brilliant Polish, Czech and Hungarian movies; the stirring theatre; the culture of samizdat; art exhibits and plays held in people's living rooms; critically oriented thinkers, intellectuals and dissidents; and great experimental books whose subversive approach was built on the tradition of the avant-garde movements of Eastern Europe. All of this has, regrettably, gone by the board, because all of it has been stymied by the same merciless stigma of 'communist' culture. There are not many today in the younger generation who know who Mikhail Bulgakov was, though his and other books have been translated, the movies have had their audiences, and artists such as Ilya Kabakov have been enshrined in Russian coffee-table picture books.

But is the stigma of communism at fault (if 'fault' is the right word) for the lack of interest? Of course not. Most of the reason for the cultural oblivion can be ascribed to the global marketplace. Global culture means the global marketplace first and foremost. The global marketplace, like any market, is guided by a simple law: survival of the fittest. Add to that the built-in reflex each of us carries, the fear of being left out. The market feeds on precisely that consumer reflex and survives therefrom. In other words, if all the kids on the block wear Nike sneakers, I, too, must wear Nike sneakers, because I do not wish to be shunted aside, right? Or, if I am a rebel, the market will find a way to commodify my rebellion, and I'll wear my anti-Nike sneakers. The young global consumer therefore devours Michel Houellebecq and considers Houellebecq the most subversive writer in the world, completely forgetting the fact that his subversive voice is being marketed in airport bookstores, in millions of copies. We live in the age of the information revolution and the global marketplace (so our consumer will wear a T-shirt with Malevich's signature on it, despite the fact that he or she will not be entirely sure who this Malevich fellow is).

The past is the favourite chewing gum of intellectuals, historians, writers and the media

Most of the guilt for cultural oblivion can be laid at the doorstep of those at work on cultural history. The hysteria around that past still goes on, the past is the favourite chewing gum of intellectuals, historians, writers, members of the Academy, the media and politicians. In Croatia, for instance, the word 'Yugoslavia' is nearly forbidden. Fifteen years ago many libraries were purged of 'communist', 'Serbian' and 'Cyrillic' books, but also other books that were considered inappropriate.

My ten-year-old friend, for instance, may not find the verse of Ivan Goran Kovačić, a fine poet, in his curriculum. Kovačić joined the partisans and was killed in the Second World War. Vladimir Nazor penned a famous onomato-poetic line of verse which every Croat knows by heart – *I cvrči cvrči cvrčak na čvoru crne smrče* (meaning: a chirping, chirping cricket on the knot of a black spruce) – which teachers of the Croatian language often foist on foreign students who are studying Croatian. (Try it! Tsvrchi, tsvrchi tscvr-chak na chvoru tsrne smrche). As they struggle with this tongue twister, foreign students have no idea that during the anti-Yugoslav and anti-communist hysteria of the early 90s there were attempts to expunge the name of Vladimir Nazor. An elderly poet at the time, Nazor had joined Tito's partisans, like Ivan Goran Kovačić, and wrote a poem celebrating Tito.

Neither of these poets is alive today. They are being rehabilitated by members of the Croatian gay movement who recently claimed that the two men had been homosexuals and lovers. The anti-communists (needless to say, everyone, today, is an anti-communist) are secretly hoping that this rehabilitation with a twist will succeed, because if it does, it will distract from the fact that the purists had tried to expunge all mention of these writers. In other words, the historical intervention of the gay community will serve to suppress the (no longer acceptable) suppression of everything communist, and make public the (now acceptable) homosexual bent of the two poets. This is only one small example of the schizophrenia of transitional, post-communist culture.

So why hasn't my ten-year-old acquaintance heard of Anne Frank?

During a recent stay in Zagreb I watched my mother's favourite morning TV show. A brief historical piece gave the story of a little girl, Lea Deutsch, an actress, 'Zagreb's little sweetheart', the 'Croatian Shirley Temple'. The pleasant voice of the speaker accompanied a sequence of photographs appearing on the screen: and then one day Lea Deutsch was put on a train headed for Auschwitz, but she never made it because she breathed her last while still on board the train. It was only last year, after so very long, that a Zagreb street was named after her. Why was that little girl put on the train? Who put her on that train? And does the fact that a street was given her name, after so very long, imply that the communists would not allow a street to be given her name? Does this mean that the street was given her name thanks to the new democratic government?

Lea Deutsch was a child actress much, indeed, like Shirley Temple, and she was Jewish. After Himmler visited Zagreb and Ante Pavelić in 1943, the Nazi government of the Independent State of Croatia put Lea Deutsch and her family on the train for Auschwitz, in order to ingratiate themselves with Himmler. And the street was given her name only now because the new government – which has at the very best only half-heartedly distanced itself from the fascism of the independent state – decided to whitewash its image a little and make it more politically correct.

Hence my concern for my dear friend, but not because he didn't know who Anne Frank was. I find myself wondering whether he will grow up to be one of the new barbarians. This will be difficult to avoid. Everyone has a stake in seeing to it: the schools, the big-name intellectuals, the historians, the politicians, television, the journalists. ... And why are they working so hard at this? Because only with new barbarians can they keep their grip on power. ❏

©Dubravka Ugresic
Translated by Ellen Elias-Bursac
40(1): 175/179
DOI: 10.1177/0306422011399703
www.indexoncensorship.org

Dubravka Ugresic's novels include *Ministry of Pain* (Saqi Books) and *Baba Yaga Laid an Egg* (Canongate). She has won numerous awards for her writing, including the Heinrich Mann Prize. 'Selective memories' will appear in a forthcoming collection of essays

179